THE
Surfcaster's Guide
TO BAITS, RIGS, AND LURES

Books by the Author

THE
Surfcaster's Guide
TO BAITS, RIGS, AND LURES

MILT ROSKO

Illustrated by Jennifer Basilio

 BURFORD BOOKS

I dedicate this book to the young people of this great land of ours. It is my heartfelt desire that their parents introduce them to the great outdoors, where they may enjoy a lifetime filled with rewarding experiences and wonderful memories.

Printed in Canada.

10 9 8 7 6 5 4 3 2

Library of Congress Cataloging-in-Publication Data

Rosko, Milt.
   The surfcaster's guide to baits, rigs & lures / Milt Rosko.
      p. cm.
Includes bibliographical references (p.   ).
   ISBN 1-58080-118-8 (pbk.)   ISBN 13   978-1-58080-118-8
1. Surf casting. 2. Fishing lures. I. Title.
   SH454.7.R67 2004
   799.1'24—dc22
                                    2003019611

Contents

ACKNOWLEDGMENTS

I've been fortunate over a span of many years to know many authors. Some penned treatises such as the one at hand, while others produced literary works of a far greater magnitude. Almost all agreed their works were a collaborative effort, with inputs from far and wide, in varying degrees of magnitude, but each important in its own way.

The very idea for this book was born as I chatted with Peter Burford, whose Burford Books published several of my earlier works. I suspect that to Peter, some of the terminology I was using sounded foreign. Quite honestly, from time to time in earlier conversations I found myself explaining each lure type, bait, or rig so he could fully understand precisely what I was referring to.

Importantly, through these many years I've been fortunate to have met, fished with, and value as my deep friends many individuals who have developed many of the lures and rigs that have become household words in the surfcasting community. I will forgo acknowledging their contributions here, because you'll find them mentioned throughout the text discussing the lures, rigs, and techniques they've helped develop, and have shared with me. They deserve my eternal gratitude, which I warmly acknowledge.

There are however, hundreds, and perhaps thousands, of surf anglers who have spent time on the beach with me, sharing the things they learned through trial and error. It's what I like about beach people. They're fine people, and I gratefully acknowledge all the help they've provided, which made writing this book pleasurable.

Very important—and I've acknowledged these two individuals in all of my prior works—are two of my teachers at West Side High in

Newark, New Jersey. Miss Rizzolo taught English, and Miss Carpenter taught typing and was our class counselor. Their encouragement and the skills they taught have lasted me a lifetime. To all the parents and grandparents who may be reading this acknowledgment, I encourage you to devote whatever it takes to ensure your children and grandchildren are in the company of fine teachers. With a quality education and family support, they'll enjoy a comfortable lifestyle.

To my granddaughter Jennifer Basilio, a sincere thank-you for the fine line drawings she prepared to illustrate this book. Jenny is a graphic-design major completing her senior year at Monmouth University. She regularly fishes with me and understands the detail necessary for her work to be helpful to fellow surfcasters.

June is my wife of 50 years, and while I'm acknowledging her last, she rightfully warrants first billing. As teenagers we fished the surf together, and we continue to fish the surf to this day. She's played a role in everything I do. Many of the photographs that accompany my articles and books are a result of her fine camera handling. She doesn't hesitate to critique my material, either, and hopefully she's made it more readable.

—Milt Rosko

INTRODUCTION

I t has been a pleasure spending a lifetime casting from the beaches of the Atlantic, Pacific, and Gulf coasts, and enjoying every moment. I am often saddened when I meet an enthusiastic surfcaster who suffers from a handicap not of his own making. So very often I've met people eager to participate in this rewarding pastime who unfortunately were given poor direction in the selection of tackle, lures, baits, and rigs and how to use them.

The misfortune of not having been tutored by an experienced angler, or having the guidance of a competent tackle shop owner, has dissuaded many folks from pursuing what could have been a rewarding lifelong avocation filled with many pleasant memories.

Often a newcomer, and even veteran caster, had nowhere to turn for definitive information on how to systematically pursue surfcasting. It was with this thought in mind that I chose to write this book. I felt that by taking you step by step from the selection of basic tackle, along with the essential accessories, on to an in-depth discussion of the variety of lures, baits, and rigs, this text would serve as a primer— a stepping-off point helping you avoid many of the distracting pitfalls so many newcomers experience.

When I began surfcasting as a preteen with my dad, there were but a handful of companies manufacturing tackle. Of the major lure types of that era, there was a very sparse selection of metal squids, plugs, and leadhead jigs. Bait rigs were limited to a hook, crude leader, swivel, and sinker.

For many years things didn't change much. Then suddenly, there was what you might call a revolution in the fishing tackle industry.

Where companies once marketed two or three models of a spinning reel, they now offered two dozen models, often confusing even the experts. The same held true for rods and lines, and the myriad accessories. When it came to lures, there were literally thousands of models, in hundreds of different finishes.

Hopefully I've included a discussion and description of all the essentials, as well as the advanced techniques, within the covers of this book. They'll enable you to pursue your surfcasting passion with a better understanding of how everything fits together and has its place in the scheme of things. No longer will you be confused between a popping plug and a surface swimming plug, a bucktail jig and a bait tail jig, or a tin squid and stainless-steel jig. The same holds true for a sand lance and spearing, and whether to use a multihook rig or a single-hook rig with these baits.

I've been most fortunate to have known and fished with some of the innovators who created and improved upon the tackle and lures discussed in this book, and I've tried to share with you some of those experiences. It is my hope that the knowledge you absorb will add to pleasant days you spend casting into the surf from our beautiful Atlantic coast beaches and help give you a lifetime of wonderful memories. Should such be the case, it will be a fitting reward for writing this book.

Selecting Surf Tackle

The single most important decision you'll make to ensure many years of enjoyable surf fishing is selecting a basic rod, reel, and line suitable to the type of casting that you plan to do. This applies to newcomer and veteran anglers alike, for I've known both to go forth ill equipped for years. Many lose interest, not realizing that in great part they were struggling and not enjoying themselves as a result of poor-quality or unbalanced tackle.

My prime recommendation to you is to seek out a reputable fishing tackle shop close to the area where you plan to do most of your fishing, or at least one familiar with the demands made on the tackle you'll be using to seek a variety of surf species. The owners of most of the shops I frequent were surf fishermen first, before getting into the tackle business. They know surf fishing, and they know fishing tackle—both important considerations.

Most of them are more than happy to spend whatever time it takes to help newcomers or veterans select an outfit suited to their style of fishing. It's what makes a happy customer. Many are pleased to take an angler out to the parking lot to try a few casts with an outfit they're recommending. You can hardly drive past the Fly Shop in Red Bank, New Jersey, without spotting a couple of anglers fly casting on the grass alongside the shop.

Down in Normandy Beach, old pro Ernie Wuesthof can regularly be seen in the parking lot of his shop, where he teaches youngsters how to cast. In fact, he regularly invites novice surf anglers to join him in his beach buggy, where the anglers can try firsthand the outfits Ernie recommends for particular applications.

There are hundreds of shops like this along the coast, and you shouldn't have any trouble finding one where the proprietor's chemistry and yours are a match. Certainly I'd recommend avoiding the discount stores, where the majority of the clerks don't know the difference between a spinning reel and a fly reel. I can't impress enough that the "surf-fishing outfit" described in the Sunday newspaper flyer may sound like a bargain, but it may be the worst possible choice for you.

When walking into a tackle shop, a newcomer is at first blush often taken aback by the masses of rods, reels, and lines that are available. I've been perplexed myself, so don't feel bad. For our purposes here, I break surfcasting outfits into the following categories:

➤ Lightweight one-handed spinning
➤ Medium-weight spinning
➤ Heavyweight spinning
➤ Lightweight one-handed multiplying
➤ Medium-weight multiplying
➤ Heavyweight multiplying
➤ Fly casting

I'm often asked what my recommendation would be for an all-around perfect choice, to which I have a pretty consistent response: For the newcomer about to enter this enjoyable pastime, the medium-weight spinning outfit will serve extremely well for a variety of applications. Going to a lighter outfit will maximize sport with smaller surf species, and when rough surf conditions dictate, it's appropriate to move up to heavier tackle.

When it comes to casting, spinning is the easiest to master. Still, the multiplying reel, while somewhat more difficult to cast, has its devotees, especially for applications such as live-bait fishing or with heavy surf conditions.

Let's take a look at the outfits sequentially, to give you some benchmarks toward making your choice.

LIGHTWEIGHT OUTFITS

The lightweight one-handed spinning outfit is an especially good choice if you're targeting the many small species that frequent the surf while using small, lightweight lures and bait. It's perfect for school stripers, tailor blues, weakfish, summer flounder, spot, croaker, and kingfish, especially when the surf is moderate and off-shore winds prevail.

Graphite rods dominate the market today, and I recommend that you select a rod made of this material: It's lighter in weight than fiberglass, it has superior power, and most of the brand names have great actions. Toward this end, spend a little time looking over the selection that's available, and by all means stick with well-known brands in all the tackle and equipment you buy. Avoid some of the cheap imports with unfamiliar brand names; most will cause you grief in the long run.

I have several one-handed spinning outfits, which range in length from 6 to 7 feet overall, some with cork grips, others with composite. Most of the rods are high-modulus graphite and have six or seven guides with a fast tip action.

Select a small saltwater spinning reel capable of holding 200 to 250 yards of 10- or 12-pound-test monofilament or fluorocarbon line. Braided lines of Spectra or Dyneema fiber feature a very fine diameter, which is only 20 percent of the diameter of monofilament lines; they're seeing increased popularity among the surfcasting fraternity. Because of their fine diameter they're more difficult to get used to than mono, so if you're a beginner, monofilament is my recommendation.

The lightweight spinning outfit is perfect for school stripers.

However, I firmly believe that braided lines—manufactured under license as Spectra in the United States and Dyneema in Europe, but of the same fiber and essentially identical—are the lines of the future. Initially they had many drawbacks, from poor knot strength, to lack of abrasion resistance, to a bad habit of digging into the spool and jamming. Because of their fine diameter and limpness, they were prone to wind knots during the cast, which often caused grief. Many of those problems have been put to rest, though, and braided lines are currently enjoying tremendous growth in the surfing community among both spinning and multiplying reel users.

Many of the smaller reels are made of graphite, withstand the onslaughts of salt water, and boast smooth ball bearings that perform flawlessly as well as drags that are smooth should you be fortunate enough to hook a heavyweight. You'll have a nicely balanced outfit, light as a feather, which will provide maximum enjoyment.

MEDIUM-WEIGHT OUTFITS

The medium-weight spinning outfit is unquestionably the most popular along the entire Atlantic coast. It's my favorite, for it's light enough to provide maximum sport with the smaller species encountered along the beach, yet has the backbone to handle the heavyweights. In all but the most severe conditions, you can punch out a good cast in heavy weather with an onshore wind.

I have several medium-weight graphite spinning rods that measure 7 to 9 feet in overall length. Some are one piece, others two piece, with seven or eight guides that distribute the strain throughout the rod. The butts are either cork, composite, or cork tape. The key is selecting a rod that can handle lures and baits from 1 to 5 ounces, which covers a rather broad range.

On this size rod I use a Penn Slammer Live Liner spinning reel. One size holds 240 yards of 12-pound-test line, while the other has a larger capacity of 260 yards of 15-pound test. The liveliner is a feature that proves very useful when fishing with live bait from surf and jetties, and is especially effective when you're bottom fishing with clams or a chunk bait and relinquish the rod to a sand spike.

The design of the reel enables you to have the regular drag system preset, with the liveliner feature allowing you to switch to a lighter drag or free spooling with the flick of a lever. I'll often fish the reel with the liveliner in position when I'm casting a live eel from the beach, or when the rod's relinquished to a sand spike. In the latter case a fish can pick up and move off with the bait with minimal drag, and as such can't pull the outfit from the sand spike. On lifting the outfit from the sand spike, the liveliner lever is disengaged and the fish can be struck using the heavier, preset drag. Once you use this feature, you'll never be without it.

What I enjoy most about using the medium-weight spinning outfit is its light weight. I know this sounds like a play on words, but when you're selecting the rod and reel, take into consideration the weight of the entire outfit. I like to fish the beach for hours on end, and I try to avoid an outfit that makes for extraneous work. It's not an exaggeration to say that within the category of the medium-weight outfit that I've just described, there can be weight differen-

Select a medium-weight rod that can handle lures from 1 to 5 ounces, but still be comfortable fishing for hours at a time.

tials of $1/2$ pound or more. The only purpose that carrying this weight serves is to minimize your enjoyment and give you a weary wrist after a couple of hours of casting.

When I reference rods throughout this chapter, I'm usually speaking of rods that have guides through which the line flows with the execution of a cast. Worth noting, however, is that rods are now being marketed where there are no guides. Instead, the line flows from the reel into the rod, where it flows through a smooth-as-silk interior, exiting through a circular tip-top. I've tried these rods, and they've worked very effectively. The only disadvantage I've seen is when you experience a line break and have to rethread through the interior of the rod. This requires using a heavier piece of monofilament as the needle with which to thread a much thinner fishing line.

When it comes to spinning reels, I am in all instances speaking of reels with a bail mechanism that is opened to execute a cast, and closes when a retrieve is begun. There are some excellent spinning reels on the market—most notably the Van Stahl—that have a manual pickup instead of a bail mechanism. Your index finger serves to lift the line from the manual pickup, after which you execute the cast and again bring your finger into play to place the line on the roller of the manual pickup. Once you've used a manual pickup, I doubt you'll want to return to the spring-activated bail, although admittedly the few reels so equipped are quite costly.

HEAVYWEIGHT OUTFITS

The heavy surf outfits are built around rods that measure 10 to 15 feet in length. They're big and heavy, and designed to cast heavy lures very long distances. Rods of this size find popularity on the beaches of Cape Cod, Block Island, Montauk, and along the Carolina Outer Banks. From my observation most anglers using rods that measure in the 13- to 15-foot range aren't really capable of handling them, because the weight of the rod is so overbearing. I know that I cannot physically handle rods of this size, and I caution you to first try some practice casting with such a rod before you purchase it. Often smaller is better.

When there's a heavy surf running and an onshore wind, the 10- to 12-foot-long models are helpful: Once you've made a cast, you're able to hold the rod up, and it will help with line control, because the line is held above the crashing waves—which isn't the case when you're using a shorter rod. Rods of this length are also great when you're fishing with the rod in a sand spike with a rough surf, for here, too, the line is held above the breaking waves.

Many of the reels marketed with the heavy surf rods are big, make no mistake about it. They're designed to be loaded with 17- to 20-pound-test line, and some anglers even spool 25-pound test for handling 8-ounce sinkers in heavy surf. The reels often have a line capacity upward of 500 yards. Some weigh more than 32 ounces. That's 2 pounds, which when combined with a 15-foot rod is just too much weight. By careful selection you can still achieve a good heavy surf outfit and reduce the overall weight by a third.

MULTIPLYING REELS

Multiplying reels also come in our three categories of light, medium, and heavy, and the rods are essentially the same overall length, only instead of spinning guides they're equipped with smaller ring guides.

The popping outfit is really designed for one-handed casting, although some of us employ two hands while using it. It's essentially a fun outfit to use while casting lures or natural baits. I use it with lures that range from 1/4 to 2 ounces in weight.

The multiplying reel has a free-spool mechanism, which automatically engages as the retrieve is begun. It features a level-wind mechanism that neatly lays the line on the reel during the retrieve. It also has a star drag feature that, when properly set, brings maximum pressure to bear on the quarry, without risking a line break.

However, properly executing a cast requires timing and delicate pressure on the line so that it doesn't overrun, causing a backlash or bird's nest. It takes a while to get used to casting with a multiplying reel, although some of the newer models have a braking mechanism that helps prevent line overruns.

In selecting a multiplying reel to balance with a light, medium, or heavy surf rod, use the same guidelines as for spinning. A reel with a capacity of 200 to 250 yards of 10- or 12-pound monofilament will work out nicely for the light popping rod, with 250 yards of 12- to 17-pound-test monofilament for the medium-weight outfit, and 400 yards of 20-pound test more than adequate for a heavy surf outfit.

Always remember the old adage that if a fish cleans you of line with any of these reels, then it certainly deserves to get away!

LEADERS

If you're using the lures and rigs that will be described later in this book, the last item of tackle is the leader. A leader of a heavier test than the line you're using is pretty much standard along the surf. The leader tends to be abused most, especially when it's often in contact with the sharp scales and gill covers of a big striper or the teeth of a bluefish.

I strongly suggest using fluorocarbon leader material between line and lure. Its refractive index is such that it's invisible in the water—a characteristic monofilament does not possess. This applies to the leaders used in tying up various rigs for use with natural baits as well.

As you'll note while perusing the balance of this book, I'm near fanatical in my use of a teaser in conjunction with a lure. Still, should you choose to just use a leader between line and lure, there are two ways you can go about it. One is to tie a surgeon's loop in the terminal end of your line, which in effect gives you a double line. This makes it easier to tie a heavier-diameter leader to the line—a loop of 15-pound test has approximately the same diameter as the 30-pound-test line it's being tied to. I've found a Venezuelan knot ideal for this purpose. It's constructed the same way as a surgeon's knot, but instead of making two overhand loops when tying, use five overhand loops and moisten the knot before pulling it up tight. This is a neat knot that can be reeled through the tip-top and guides with ease. At the terminal end of the leader, use a uniknot to tie a duolock snap and you're all set.

Another option, which some anglers favor, is to use a tiny 50-pound-test Spro power swivel between line and leader. Use a surgeon's loop at the terminal end of the line and then a uniknot to tie it to the swivel, with another uniknot to tie the leader to the duolock snap.

FLY CASTING

Fly casting has taken the surf by storm in recent years. I suspect it's been an evolutionary process for some, who enjoy using the long rod to present a tiny bit of feathers to the wide variety of species that call the surf their home. Admittedly the surf is a tough saltwater environment to fish with a fly rod, especially when compared to most boat-casting situations.

I've made it a point to always have a fly rod close at hand, whether I'm driving the beach in a beach buggy or just carrying a rigged-up rod in the car. I seldom try to use the fly rod when there's an onshore wind—the surf is often so rough, and the wind so strong, as to make casting unmanageable. However, when there's light or little wind, and I know from having caught stripers, blues, weaks, summer flounder, or little tunny that the likelihood is good these species will be raiding the beach, then I'll opt for the fly rod, as both a challenge and a change of pace.

My favorite fly rod for times when the smaller surf species are most abundant is an 8-weight measuring 9 feet in overall length, with a 400-grain sinking fly line, spooled on a reel with 200 yards of backing. This is light and easy to use, and I can walk along the sand with a stripping basket strapped around my waist and cast to my heart's content.

I always have a fly rod close at hand. When decent-sized stripers such as this one are in the area, I'll opt for a 9- or 10-weight outfit.

When stripers in the teens or alligator blues topping the 12-pound mark are known to be in the area, I'll opt for a 9- or 10-weight outfit, often switching to a floating line when blues, stripers, or little tunny are chasing forage on the surface, which allows me to fish a popping bug and enjoy surface strikes. I must say, however, that overall the high-density sinking line consistently brings more strikes than does working a popping bug or surface slider.

For the most part I employ a relatively short leader—half the length of normal fly leaders—with just 6 feet of fluorocarbon, tapering in equal lengths of 30-, 20-, and 15-pound test, with a titanium tippet in the event bluefish are plentiful.

When it comes to flies, I'd begin with a selection of five patterns as described later in this book. Master their use and you'll be far ahead of the anglers who go forth with hundreds of patterns and spend more time changing flies than they do fishing them.

Much of what I've said about selecting a spinning or multiplying surf outfit applies to a fly-casting outfit as well, only more so. Balance is the key ingredient with each outfit. Take the time to find a shopkeeper dedicated to serving your needs and level of experience, even if you've been fishing for many years. The kinds of tips and coaching they can offer will go a long way to making your days and nights along the beach most enjoyable. Of that I'm certain.

HOOKS

Anglers fishing the surf use a variety of hooks in seeking their favorite game fish and bottom feeders. Some are an integral part of lures, while others are designed expressly for use with natural baits. Some, like the popular O'Shaughnessy style, may be effectively used with lures or natural bait. While a review of hook catalogs will disclose literally hundreds of styles and sizes, the surf angler can prudently narrow this list down to eight models, and can be assured that they will perform effectively in the great majority of situations encountered.

I've been selective in the hooks I use, and the accompanying illustrations include those of which I have a high regard:

O'Shaughnessy

I suspect that the O'Shaughnessy style would qualify as the single best all-around hook that can effectively be used with lures or natural baits. It's constructed of heavy wire, which penetrates well and holds securely when used in lure construction, such as with metal squids and leadheads. The O'Shaughnessy is also very effective when used with a variety of natural baits, ranging from clams to live mackerel or herring.

Live Bait

The Live Bait–style hook has a shorter shank, and its point is bent in, when compared to the O'Shaughnessy. It's favored by anglers who use live menhaden, herring, mackerel, spot, or other forage species, enabling them to hook the bait either through the back just forward of the dorsal fin, or through the lips. Because of its small size it is inconspicuous and enables a baitfish to swim unencumbered.

Claw or Beak

The Claw- and Beak-style hooks are very similar in design, and are without question the most popular style used while bottom fishing with natural baits from the surf. They are available with a regular eye, and a turned-down or turned-up eye, and lend themselves well to use with spearing, sand eels, live mummichog, shrimp, and chunks or strips of bait such as squid.

Claw or Beak with Baitholder Shank

Claw- or Beak-style hooks are available with a barbed baitholder shank. This proves helpful when using bait that tends to ball up on the hook. When using sandworms or bloodworms, the worm is threaded onto the hook then pushed up onto the shank, where the barbed baitholder shank holds it in place. The baitholder shank also proves effective when threading a piece of clam meat onto the hook, or any of the popular chunk baits cut from butterfish, mackerel, or herring.

Wide Gap or Kahle

The Wide Gap hook finds popularity on bottom rigs designed for kingfish, scup, spot, croaker, weakfish, and fluke. It has fine hooking qualities when combined with the wide variety of natural baits used to seek bottom feeders. By virtue of its design—the eye and point are on the same plane—the hook usually penetrates farther back in the fish's mouth. Its long shank makes unhooking a fish relatively easy.

Circle

The Circle-style hook dates back centuries, for it is an extremely effective hook that requires practically no effort on the part of the angler to hook a fish. By its very design, when a fish inhales a bait placed on a Circle hook, the bait can literally be swallowed and will usually not penetrate in the mouth or stomach; instead, as the fish turns to swim away, the hook begins to exit and usually lodges in the corner of the fish's jaw. The Circle style has become extremely popular among striped bass fishermen in particular, and especially those who fish with clams as bait, for the fish are not injured and can easily be unhooked and released. The hook's popularity has grown to the point that some states now note in their regulations that Circle-style hooks must be used when fishing for certain species. This is particularly true for species where size limits are in effect, and undersized fish have to be released unharmed.

Treble

This is the standard Treble style hook most often found on plugs, although some manufacturers also place them on metal squids and jigs. By its very design it is effective on plugs, for fish strike at the lure and are impaled by the free-swinging hooks. The problem rests with the unhooking of a fish. Many game fish are now regulated with respect to size, bag, and season limits, and care must be exercised in unhooking them. I continue to use trebles on plugs, but change all of my tin squids, stainless-steel jigs, and chromed spoons to carry a single O'Shaughnessy-style hook, which facilitates release without harming the fish.

Triple-Grip Treble

The Triple-Grip Treble is a relatively new design in treble hooks, and has the best hooking quality of any treble I've ever used. I regularly rehang lures that come equipped with standard trebles, replacing them with the Triple-Grip style. I then go another step and use a pair of pliers to bend down the barbs. The Triple-Grip design, coupled with the bent-down barbs, ensures excellent holding quality once a fish is hooked, and it makes for ease in unhooking and releasing game fish without injury.

Surf Accessories and Equipment

I t's a beautiful late-summer evening as you walk along a picturesque stretch of beach. The sunbathers are gone, and where they once frolicked in the surf the terns are picking anchovies from the surface. Suddenly what you've waited all summer for happens: The surf erupts in feeding bluefish.

You cast, slapping a mosquito carried to the beach with the offshore wind that brought them from the mainland. Immediately you're hooked up, and between a screeching reel drag and bucking rod, you slap another mosquito and then another. Finally you walk into the surf waist deep to avoid the attack of the pesky critters. You can't enjoy the fishing, which is the best of the season, and by the time you retreat your arms and neck are full of welts. *Oh, why did I forget the insect repellent!*

Properly equipping yourself with a balanced outfit for the exciting pastime of surf fishing is a great beginning. In subsequent chapters I hope to tell you about some of the baits, rigs, and lures that will enhance your opportunity to enjoy the beach, much as June and I have enjoyed it these many years. In between, however, are myriad small, seemingly insignificant items—a squeeze bottle of insect repellent, or a headlamp as darkness sets in and the stripers turn on—without which an otherwise eventful trip turns into something less than enjoyable.

STAYING MOBILE: VESTS, PACKS, AND BAGS

By its very nature surf fishing is most enjoyable when you can move about and enjoy the beauty of the beach, unencumbered by excessive gear. Mobility is the key. While certain situations, such as live-bait fishing, require cumbersome gear, you want to plan your surf-fishing excursions so that you're self-contained. You want to be able to walk for a mile or two, all the while carrying everything you need with ease.

There are several approaches you can employ. I've opted for using a fly-fishing vest as I walk the beach; its many pockets enable me to carry all that I'll need. Admittedly, at times the pockets bulge with a wide variety of must-have gear, but seldom is there a time when I don't have everything I need.

I generally wear a fly-fishing vest as I surfcast on the beach. Its many pockets allow me to carry everything I'll need.

The fly-fishing vest is really a compromise, for they're designed for freshwater fishing. Often I've thought of designing a saltwater angler's surf vest, and persuading a company to manufacture it. It'd have pockets better designed to hold the bigger lures and accessories that I like to carry.

Far and away the most popular way of carrying the gear you need is to use a shoulder bag. Most shoulder bags are designed to hold 8 to 10 saltwater plugs, which are carried in tubes located in the bag to keep them from tangling. There are several pockets with Velcro closures that accommodate metal squids, leadhead jigs, leaders, teasers, and assorted other items. I've found most of them to be too large, and as a result I tend to fill them up with items I seldom use. The net result is often a tired back and shoulder after a night on the beach. The shoulder bag is, however, certainly more practical than taking a tackle box to the beach.

Tackle boxes are made for boat fishermen, not surf fishermen. The exception is that I keep a big Plano tackle box in the trunk of my car or in my beach buggy, so that backup items are always readily available. When it's full the box weighs a lot, and it certainly isn't something I'd ever carry to the beach.

Another unique approach to carrying gear is to wear a fanny pack. Plano has such a pack that I've used from time to time, although by its very nature it's limited in the amount of terminal tackle it holds. It has an expandable belt that neatly clips together around your waist and is comfortable to wear.

SUNGLASSES

Some of the finest surf fishing takes place early in the morning—often as the blazing sun pops up on the horizon. This can be very uncomfortable to look into, so intense are its rays. I've found that a pair of Polaroid sunglasses not only makes for more comfortable fishing but also gives me the decided advantage of being able to observe baitfish, the dimples of feeding fish, and other activity that I might otherwise overlook.

REPELLENT

Then there's the matter of insect repellent. If the wind's onshore you won't have a problem, because it'll blow the green flies, mosquitoes, and other biting critters back toward land. Irrespective of wind direction, I always carry the smallest squeeze bottle of insect repellent that's available. I really prefer the spray can, but it's bulkier to carry. I've been thankful to have it along on many occasions, and equally irritated when I failed to include it in my vest pockets.

SAND SPIKES

A sand spike is a useful tool in certain types of surf fishing. It's a 3-foot-long plastic tube with a 2-inch diameter; its pointed end is easily pushed into the sand, and the other end accommodates your rod. If I plan to use lures when working a stretch of beach, I don't carry a sand spike. It's not needed—if I want to change lures or un-hook a fish, I just lean the rod against my shoulder.

If I'm bait fishing, however, I always carry a sand spike. It holds the rod when I'm cutting bait and baiting up. Often I'll fish a pair of rods from a pair of sand spikes, casting one bait far from the beach and the other in close, a technique designed to intercept any game fish or bottom feeders moving along the beach.

Longer is better than shorter: I've seen 2-foot-long sand spikes that were easily pulled over when a fish picked up a baited hook and

Most of what I'll need for a morning of surfcasting: rods and reels, surf bag with lures, lure wallets with metal jigs and spoons, insect repellent, headlamp, measuring tape, pliers, and a bait knife.

moved off, dragging the rod and reel from the sand spike and into the surf. The past couple of seasons prior to my writing this book we had a huge run of bullnose rays along the coast, and I suspect they dragged off dozens of rods and reels that anglers felt were secure in their sand spikes.

If you don't have a reel with a liveliner feature, which permits you to fish with little or no drag, overriding the primary drag, by all means back off on your reel's drag when it's in a sand spike so it doesn't get pulled into the surf.

Sometimes you'll find the sand packed so hard that it's difficult to push your sand spike sufficiently deep. I've found that pushing it in as far as I can, and then literally sitting on the end of the sand spike with my full body weight, accompanied by a couple of up-and-down bumps with my bottom, usually pushes the spike sufficiently deep.

KNIVES AND CUT BAIT

For bait fishing you'll most certainly require a knife to cut bait. Many anglers carry a huge sheath knife that's big enough to butcher a hog, which is not only cumbersome but also unnecessary. I've settled on a 4-inch-long stainless-steel single-bladed pocketknife made by Buck Knives. It's more than adequate for cutting bait; I've even shucked clams with it, and cleaned fish as well. I regularly hone its edge at home, and its pen-type clip holds it securely in a pocket of my fly vest, always available.

Many of the baits you'll use while surf fishing have to be cut, and nothing can be more frustrating than being on the beach and having a sharp knife, but no cutting board. I've settled on a 4- by 6- by 1-inch piece of teak that's just big enough to cut strips from squid, chunk baits from menhaden or herring, or pieces of clam or soft crab.

Some baits tend to be soft even when fresh, including soft calico, blue, or rock crabs, and clams; if you place them on the hook they'll often rip free during the cast. Always bring a small spool of elastic thread with you when you're fishing these baits, taking several turns of the thread around the bait and tying it off securely. It'll save the frustration of cutting a nice bait, then watching it sail to the horizon as you execute a cast.

I religiously make it a point to avoid taking the plastic bags or cardboard boxes in which frozen baits are packaged to the beach. Too often I've seen anglers discard these containers on the beach, and I've even had them inadvertently blow away in the wind. Instead I take a few minutes back at the house to remove the baits and place them in a 1-quart margarine container with a secure lid, or a comparable-sized plastic pickle jar. This keeps the bait neat and moist, and is easily transported. Handling and cutting bait can be messy at times, so it's always wise to carry a hand towel as well.

I carry with me a 6-foot-long piece of ¹/₈-inch nylon rope in which I've tied a loop that fits over my shoulder. To the other end of the rope I tie a small metal snap. I can adjust the rope in such a fashion as to drag a couple of big fish along the sand, with the snap and rope threaded through their gills and then doubled back on the line. I can also adjust the loop on the rope to secure half a dozen or so smaller fish, which are carried at waist level as I move about. Easy and convenient, especially if I'm using lures and am a mile or more from the car. I also carry a small plastic bag, which can easily accomodate several small fish.

PLASTIC BUCKETS

Along about now you may be wondering how I carry all this to the beach. I use a 5-gallon plastic bucket, complete with cover. I use a

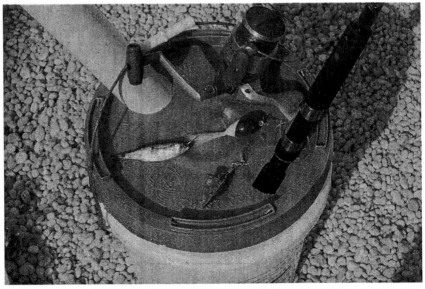

Properly adapted, a 5-gallon plastic bucket makes a terrific carryall for fishing the beach.

2 1/2-inch doorknob hole cutter to cut a neat hole on each side of the lid. Once the bucket is filled with all the aforementioned items, I put the lid on, raise the handle to secure it, and finally add two sand spikes, which I insert through the holes.

Lest I forget, I use a tool organizer in the bottom of the bucket. They're available at hardware outlets, and are used by carpenters primarily to separate the various nails and small items they use. Most have four compartments and a handle, and neatly fit into the bottom of the 5-gallon bucket. I use one compartment for sinkers, another for rigs, one for bait, and one for towel, elastic thread, bait-cutting board, and a rope stringer to carry my catch.

I repair to the beach with the bucket and its sand spikes and related gear in one hand, and a pair of rods and reels in the other. I'm all set to spend an enjoyable day at the beach, complete with everything I'll ever need.

Because surf fishing with natural baits is often a waiting game, it can be tiresome, and the bait bucket, with its cover on, makes a perfect seat as you wait for a hungry game fish or bottom feeder to happen by.

HEADLAMP

One of the most important pieces of equipment that I use is a miner's headlamp. So many anglers I know fail to wear their light, then find themselves on the beach before first light amid a feeding frenzy of stripers, blues, or channel bass—and miss out on most of the action because they can't see what they're doing. Just trying to undo a line loop or backlash becomes impossible. Likewise, many anglers who fish toward dusk fail to carry a light. Just at dark the fish turn on, but these fishermen are stuck fumbling as they try to remove a pair of treble hooks from the jaw of a frisky adversary flopping around on the beach. Even if I leave for the beach two hours before dark, I always put on my light. Locally, people think the light and I are attached!

Speaking of attaching the light, most miner's-style headlamps come equipped with a cumbersome rubber belt that is designed to be placed on your head, or on your hat, as the case may be. I've found this annoying, because pressure is what holds the light in place. To solve the dilemma, my daughter Linda sewed a piece of strapping from an old fanny pack to the brackets of the light. The strap has a plastic snap connector, and I strap the light around my neck. It fits comfortably, and I can easily direct its beam when landing a big fish in the surf or tying a knot with fine braided line. The light has four A-cell batteries and an excellent beam.

I suggest avoiding a handheld flashlight; most often you're doing things with both hands. I also don't like the small handheld-style flashlights that some anglers wear around their necks, and then put in their mouths as they work with their hands. Having tried a variety of lights, I've for many years settled on the miner's headlamp style as best for surf and jetty work.

Speaking of lights, there's a neat rod-tip light that's just great when you're night fishing. Called the Breakaway Old Red Eye, it's a small battery-powered light that easily slips onto the tip of a surf rod. Often I'll fish with clams or chunk baits at night, utilizing a pair of outfits that I place in sand spikes. The tiny red lights are clearly visible as I sit and wait for a strike. When a fish picks up the bait, the

A headlamp is one of the most important pieces of equipment in the surfcaster's arsenal. I like to wear mine around my neck rather than strapped to the head.

movement of the red light on the rod tip is clearly visible, alerting me to get there quickly!

BOOTS AND WADERS

Surf footwear ranges from sandals to chest waders. Chest waders are admittedly bulky and uncomfortable to wear, but for all-around use throughout the entire season they're your best bet for fishing the beach, especially if you do a lot of night fishing, and particularly if you fish heavy surf.

For summer or warm-weather areas many surfcasters use stockingfoot waders in conjunction with a lace-up bootfoot. If you prefer an insulated wader, look toward neoprene bootfoot models with a rubber sole. They'll keep you plenty warm in even severe weather, but you'll perspire in them during summer.

Korkers, shown here strapped to my wader boots, are essential safety equipment when fishing groins or jettys.

I used knee boots and hip boots years ago, but invariably had a particularly big wave push well up the beach and go over the top of them.

I especially like the summer months, when I can wade the surf with a bathing suit or pair of shorts. You've got to wait until the water temperatures reach 70 degrees, after which it's very comfortable to either go barefoot or use a pair of water shoes. The new water shoes are made of neoprene and two-way stretch material, which ensures that the shoes stay on your feet even when you're awash in the surf. They're especially comfortable if you fish beaches with a lot of rocks, shells, or other debris.

Should you venture onto the groins and jetties that extend seaward along the coast, make certain to strap a pair of Korkers to your boots. Korkers have a series of carbide spikes that ensure secure footing on even the most slippery rocks, and they hold especially well on the mussels that cover many rocks that are exposed at low tide. A new model of Korkers is built into an ankle boot, which is ideal if you fish exclusively from groins and jetties and don't have to wade.

You can also wear a pair of golf shoes with aluminum studs. The key is to avoid wearing sneakers or other smooth-soled footwear whenever you traverse a groin or jetty. The rocks are often covered with marine growth, which is slippery, and if your footing isn't secure you can end up severely injured.

OTHER ESSENTIALS

How many times have you nicked yourself when removing a hook from a toothy jaw, or received a cut from a sharp gill cover? Nothing is more annoying than a cut that keeps bleeding. I regularly carry three or four Band-Aids in a tiny plastic holder. Not only have I used them regularly, but over the years I've also provided fellow anglers with these tiny strips that solve the bleeding problem and help prevent infection.

Of course you can often avoid some of those cuts and nicks by carrying a good pair of long-nosed pliers. The long-nosed models are especially effective when removing the hooks from deep-hooked toothy adversaries, as well as when handling plug-hooked fish.

Those multiuse folding tools consisting of pliers, knife, screwdriver, and sundry other tool heads are also effective and certainly good to carry if you prefer but a single tool.

A retractable nail clipper or scissor attached to your jacket or fly vest will do yeoman service during the season. I make it a practice to cut back the terminal end of my line, then retie it on each sojourn to the beach, because the terminal end and knots take the greatest punishment while fishing from the sand. A clipper makes trimming the knots neat and effortless.

Another retractable item I carry is a tape measure. It's a 1 1/2-inch-diameter model, and is a must on the beach, because state regulations with respect to size are in effect on so many surf species. A tape measure enables you to immediately determine whether or not a fish may be kept.

I also carry a single small sheet of the regulations of the state I'm fishing in tucked into my vest. At the beginning of the season I cut it out of *The Fisherman* magazine, which has a complete list. Given the wide range of seasons, bag limits, and size limits in effect—all of which vary from state to state—it's best to know what the regulations are and then to abide by them. I've observed individuals who landed fish and then were in a quandary as to whether or not they could keep them.

Casual surf anglers are occasionally issued a summons for being in violation of the fish and game code. Many of these folks just weren't aware that they were in violation—they were simply tourists out for a day of enjoyment.

Often the best surf fishing is experienced in the worst weather, especially when there's a strong onshore wind gusting that can literally send sheets of water toward you. That's when foul-weather gear comes into play. Keep a lightweight rain parka available; when you arrive at your favorite surfing destination you can slip into it if the wind's out of an easterly quarter. It sure beats being showered with windswept spray.

All of these accessories and equipment will add to your enjoyment of surf fishing. Initially it may sound like a big undertaking to get all of this gear together, but once you've assembled and organized it, you'll find you're totally mobile. It's really an important consideration when you choose to seek the wide variety of game fish and bottom dwellers that move along the tumbling surf to feed.

Surfcaster's Checklist

- Fly-fishing vest
- Shoulder bag
- Lure pouch
- Fanny pack
- Polaroid sunglasses
- Insect repellent
- Sand spike
- Pocketknife
- Hand towel
- Cutting board
- Plastic bait container
- Plastic rope to carry fish
- Small plastic bag
- Bait and tackle organizer
- Miner's headlamp
- Battery-powered rod light
- Band-Aids
- Multipurpose tool
- Long-nosed pliers
- Retractable nail clipper
- State fishing regulations
- Waders
- Spiked footwear for jetties
- Rain parka

CHAPTER 3

Surfman's Knots

So many times I've heard surf anglers tell of hooking a "good one that broke the line." The fact of the matter is that the line proper seldom breaks; most line breaks can be attributed to improperly tied knots. The accompanying knot illustrations are all you'll need to know to be successful when fishing the surf, and work well with monofilament and braided line.

The uniknot is my favorite, and I regularly employ it whenever I attach line to a leader, to a swivel, or to the eye of a hook. It can also be used to join two lines. It has excellent knot strength.

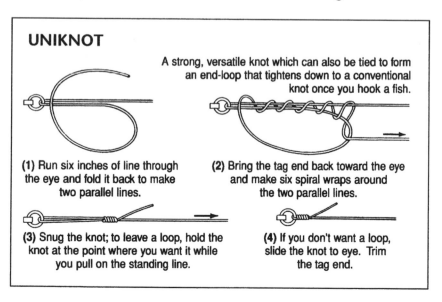

UNIKNOT

A strong, versatile knot which can also be tied to form an end-loop that tightens down to a conventional knot once you hook a fish.

(1) Run six inches of line through the eye and fold it back to make two parallel lines.

(2) Bring the tag end back toward the eye and make six spiral wraps around the two parallel lines.

(3) Snug the knot; to leave a loop, hold the knot at the point where you want it while you pull on the standing line.

(4) If you don't want a loop, slide the knot to eye. Trim the tag end.

JOINING LINES

THE UNIKNOT SYSTEM

1. Overlap ends of two lines of about same diameter for about 6". With one end, form Uni-Knot

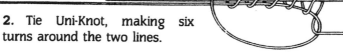

circle, crossing the two lines about midway of overlapped distance.

2. Tie Uni-Knot, making six turns around the two lines.

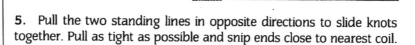

3. Pull tag end to snug knot tight around line.

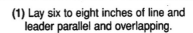

4. Use loose end of overlapped line to tie another Uni-Knot and snug up.

5. Pull the two standing lines in opposite directions to slide knots together. Pull as tight as possible and snip ends close to nearest coil.

SURGEON'S KNOT

This easy-to-tie knot is popular for joining a heavy monofilament leader to a lighter monofilament main line.

(1) Lay six to eight inches of line and leader parallel and overlapping.

(2) Using the two lines, tie an overhand knot.

(3) Proceed to tie a second overhand knot.

(4) Pull both lines in opposing directions to gather and tighten the knot. Trim tag ends.

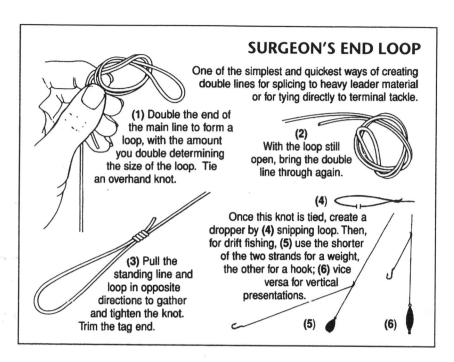

SURGEON'S END LOOP

One of the simplest and quickest ways of creating double lines for splicing to heavy leader material or for tying directly to terminal tackle.

(1) Double the end of the main line to form a loop, with the amount you double determining the size of the loop. Tie an overhand knot.

(2) With the loop still open, bring the double line through again.

(3) Pull the standing line and loop in opposite directions to gather and tighten the knot. Trim the tag end.

Once this knot is tied, create a dropper by **(4)** snipping loop. Then, for drift fishing, **(5)** use the shorter of the two strands for a weight, the other for a hook; **(6)** vice versa for vertical presentations.

I often double the last couple of feet of the terminal end of my line using a surgeon's loop. This is a neat yet strong loop that has worked extremely well for me. I then use a uniknot to tie the loop to the swivel.

The surgeon's knot is effective when joining two lines together, especially your backing to your primary line. A modification is the Venezuelan knot, which passes the line through the loop five times, and is very strong.

The improved clinch knot is also a strong knot. Many surf anglers prefer it for attaching a lure or rig.

The dropper loop is ideal when making up leaders with which you'll have a teaser. It also works extremely well when tying up a two-hook bottom rig: The loop can be tied to the desired size, and the hooks slipped right onto it. I regularly use it when tying my favorite two-hook bottom rig.

Knowing how to properly snell a hook comes in handy when you want to tie your own rigs. The Snelling a Hook illustration will prove helpful in this regard.

Some surfmen have turned to using titanium wire, which can be tied with regular knots to attach the wire to a swivel. If you want to make a direct link between line and titanium leader, you'll find the spider hitch works extremely well.

If you're going to use stainless-steel wire, use the haywire twist. This combination of twisting the wire haywire fashion, then finishing off with a barrel twist and breaking cleanly, makes a perfect connection.

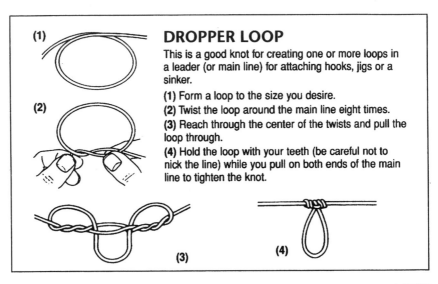

DROPPER LOOP

This is a good knot for creating one or more loops in a leader (or main line) for attaching hooks, jigs or a sinker.

(1) Form a loop to the size you desire.

(2) Twist the loop around the main line eight times.

(3) Reach through the center of the twists and pull the loop through.

(4) Hold the loop with your teeth (be careful not to nick the line) while you pull on both ends of the main line to tighten the knot.

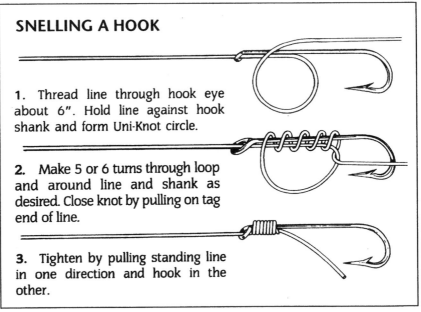

SNELLING A HOOK

1. Thread line through hook eye about 6". Hold line against hook shank and form Uni-Knot circle.

2. Make 5 or 6 turns through loop and around line and shank as desired. Close knot by pulling on tag end of line.

3. Tighten by pulling standing line in one direction and hook in the other.

BLOOD KNOT

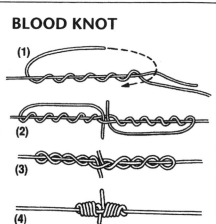

One of the best knots for splicing two monofilament lines of similar diameter — or for joining two dissimilar-diameter lines by doubling the lighter of the two.

(1) Overlap the two parallel lines by 12 inches total. Take five wraps on one side and pull the end back through between the two strands.

(2) Repeat on the other side, pulling the other end through the strands in the opposite direction.

(3) Pull the two tag ends slowly to gather the knot, and **(4)** once gathered neatly, pull the standing line to tighten the knot. Trim the tag ends.

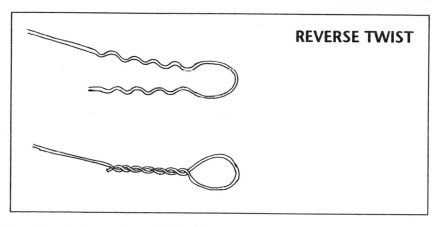

REVERSE TWIST

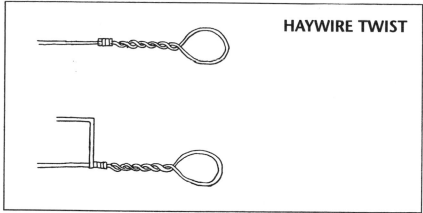

HAYWIRE TWIST

Many anglers prefer using a reverse-twist wire connection when using lures, because this enables them to easily change lures without having to use a snap. It takes a bit of patience to reverse-twist the wire, but once you've acquired the knack you'll find it very effective.

The best way to master knots and wire connections is through practice at home. All of these knots should look neat and smooth when finished. Spend a couple of evenings with the illustrations and work at tying the knots until you're comfortable. One last thought: Always cut back a couple of feet of line after a day of fishing, and begin your next trip with new knots.

CHAPTER 4

Terminal Tackle

A s I walk the beach, I often happen upon an angler who just recently started surf fishing. The first giveaway that he's a newcomer is that he carries a tackle box to the beach. A glance at his gear usually tells me he visited a discount chain store and was sold mass-merchandised rigs that looked as though they were designed to decorate a Christmas tree!

I like to stop and chat a while when I make this observation, for right from the start the angler is working under a handicap. Frequently I've been able to provide some guidance, and often I've helped an angler modify his rigs to better suit the fishing opportunities at hand. Over the years I suspect I've given anglers on the beach a hundred or more fluke rigs—I'd be catching the flatfish when they couldn't get a hit. I enjoy doing this because it results in the angler not only catching fish and enjoying his day, but also quickly learning how important proper terminal rigging is.

The mass-merchandised rigs I alluded to above are made with huge snap swivels, oversized three-way swivels, beads, feathers, sinker snaps . . . they're really just too much clutter. Most of the swivels are of a size and test that would be appropriate for tuna fishing, not seeking the quarry found in the surf.

More than anything else, the best advice I can offer with respect to terminal tackle is, *Keep it plain and keep it simple.* Throughout this book there'll be descriptions of fine-quality lures, baits, and rigs. Almost without exception you'll detract from their effectiveness when you use too much terminal tackle to present these lures. Indeed, I've seen anglers using 1/2-ounce plugs that were connected to a huge snap swivel almost as long as the plug! To say the snap swivel detracted from the lure's action would be an understatement. In addition, you must remember that you're trying to seduce a fish into striking your lure, so it certainly isn't warranted to adorn it with extraneous hardware that could conceivably spook a fish at the last moment.

When selecting ready-made rigs, I suggest you stop by a local tackle shop and seek the counsel of the proprietor. Many shops tie their own rigs, using top-grade components geared for the fishing and species encountered in their particular area.

If you decide to tie your own terminal rigs and leaders, then avoid the economy-grade loose swivels and snaps. You can't go wrong choosing brands such as Spro, Rosco, or Sampo—they've been in business for a long while and make quality components. As for hooks, look for Eagle Claw, Mustad, Owner, Gamakatsu, VMC, and Daiichi, all of which produce state-of-the-art hooks with laser-sharp points and chemically treated metal that withstands the onslaught of salt water and its corrosive action.

I can't stress enough that you should avoid sharpening a new hook. Years ago I was the first to recommend using a file to sharpen a hook right out of the box, because back then brand-new hooks literally weren't sharp. That's not the case today. Now technology is such that all the above manufacturers are providing anglers with excellent hook designs and points that are sharp enough to ensure quick penetration and holding strength.

Despite the quality finishes on hooks, they're still bound to rust after prolonged use in salt water. This applies to both single hooks on bait rigs and the treble and single hooks found on lures. My attitude with a rusty hook is that it belongs in the trash can. I regularly discard hooks, and have spare trebles and singles that are easily slipped in place with the aid of a split-ring plier and stainless-steel split rings.

Believe me when I say you will be well served to follow my practice of making it a rule that rusty hooks belong in the trash, for it'll save you the anguish of missing a strike when a rusty hook won't penetrate—or worse still, of losing a big one because the hook broke as a result of being weakened by rust.

I also caution you that to prolong the life of your terminal tackle, rigs, and lures, store them in a well-ventilated place on returning from the beach. Avoid leaving them in a closed surf bag in the trunk of your car, where they can't dry out, and they'll last much longer and provide trouble-free performance.

TERMINAL TACKLE ESSENTIALS

There are only half a dozen items of terminal tackle that you'll find useful in your quest of surf species. They're important, however. Although small, the weakest link in the chain can cause you grief. The weakest link can often be a swivel, a snap, or even a sinker, all of which cost but pennies.

I make mention of this because there is a tremendous amount of very poor-quality terminal gear on the market. Don't think a swivel is just a swivel, or a snap is just a snap. Purchase major brands and avoid all bulk snaps and swivels. Never, but never purchase a snap that doesn't have a curved locking mechanism. I can almost guarantee failure on a big fish.

Small barrel swivels are most often employed as a connection between your line and leader. Shortly after I became aware of them, I became a believer in Spro power swivels, which are barrel swivels one and a half times stronger for their size than any comparable swivels. The tiny size 8 tests at 50 pounds, and the size 6 tests at 80 pounds. Both are ideal for surf work.

Some anglers make the mistake of using a snap swivel between line and leader, which in my view is cumbersome and a waste.

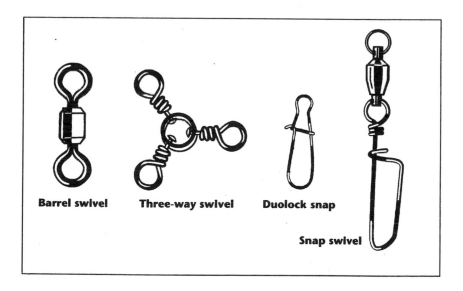

Barrel swivel   **Three-way swivel**   **Duolock snap**

Snap swivel

The duolock-style snap is ideal for changing lures. It's made of a single piece of formed wire, rounded on both ends, with a sure-lock mechanism that locks around itself, ensuring that it won't open at an inopportune time. I usually use the 1/2-inch models for attaching small flies and teasers, moving on up to 1 inch at the end of the leader for lures.

Three-way swivels are popular for use when bottom fishing. Your line is attached to one eye of the swivel, the sinker or sinker snap to another, and the leader to the remaining eye. For most surf-fishing applications, stick with size 2 or 1/0, because they're small and strong.

In lieu of a three-way swivel many surf anglers opt for a duolock sinker slide. The line is slipped through a small plastic sleeve, which has a duolock snap attached to it, onto which your sinker is snapped. When a fish picks up your bait and moves off with it, there's no sinker resistance.

Far and away the most popular sinker employed by surf anglers is the pyramid style. This four-sided sinker holds very well in heavy surf. Keep a selection ranging from 1 to 6 ounces in your surf bag.

Gaining in popularity among surf anglers is the breakaway-style sinker. These have sinker arms that collapse under force, which makes retrieving them along a sand bottom easier than with a pyramid model.

For those occasions when you're casting and retrieving a bait, such as with a Sneaky Pete rig for flounder, you'll find either a dipsey-style sinker with a swivel eye or a bank-style sinker ideal. Carry weights ranging from 1/2 through 3 ounces and you'll be set for most surf situations.

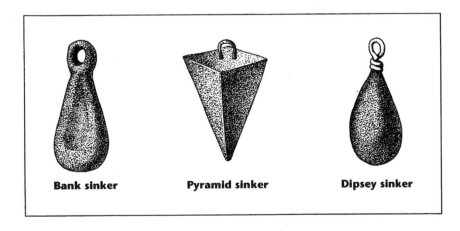

Bank sinker   **Pyramid sinker**   **Dipsey sinker**

CHAPTER 5

Lures

There is a wide array of lures designed to catch fish in the surf. Keep in mind that for each lure type described here, there are literally hundreds of models produced by various manufacturers, each with nuances that are said to add to its fish-catching effectiveness.

Of late rattle chambers have come into vogue; plug manufacturers attempt to have their rattles produce the same sounds as the forage species the plug represents. Aerodynamics even plays a role —shapes are designed to minimize wind resistance while casting. The soft plastic tails of leadhead jigs now feature chum chambers that result in the lure giving off a scent of the chum as it's retrieved. Among saltwater flies, the magnitude of patterns is mind-boggling. At one time or another each and every one of the lures discussed herein will catch fish.

Begin with a nominal selection. The key is mastering each of the lure types that you carry to the beach with you. Avoid going forth with a surf bag loaded with a couple of dozen lures, making a cast or two, and then changing lures. Not only do you waste a lot of time, but more often than not you're not effectively using the lure and learning what it takes to fish it properly.

Keep in mind you'll be most successful in mastering each of these lures independently of the others. Learn how to use them and under what conditions they're most appropriate. Most often you'll settle upon a trusted few and enjoy great fishing.

Surface Swimmer

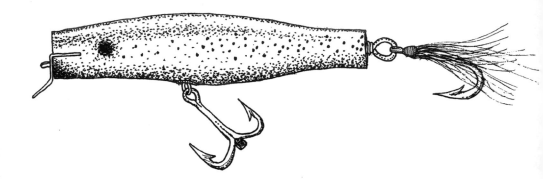

The surface swimmer is among the most exciting plugs to use, for as it is retrieved it swims enticingly within sight. When game fish charge the plug, every strike is a new experience. Some fish strike as though it's the last food in the sea, others swirl behind it repeatedly before making a decision, some just suck it into their mouths, while still others go airborne and crash down on it. Each gives the angler an adrenaline rush like no other!

MODELS

You'll find a number of manufacturers that produce surface swimmers. Among the most popular for more than half a century has been the Bob Pond Atom plug. Originally made of wood, but now of a plastic that floats, the Atom is available from tiny 3-inch-long models on up to those measuring 8 inches, in a variety of finishes that resemble the wide range of forage found along the coast.

I've long been partial to wooden surface swimming plugs turned of cedar, because they have superior flotation. I'm especially partial to the Danny plug, now manufactured by Gibbs Lures. The surface swimmer has a near-vertical metal lip, which gives it a side-to-side swimming action when retrieved. It should always stay right on top—the result of its spoonlike or flat lip, which doesn't pull it beneath the surface.

FISHING THE LURE

A great deal of discipline is required to use the surface swimmer properly. It provides maximum effectiveness when retrieved slowly, very slowly. Many anglers make the mistake of retrieving it too fast, in a mechanical manner. You want it to just lazily swim along, much like an unsuspecting menhaden, mullet, herring, or other forage. Always keep in mind that stripers, blues, weaks, channel bass, tarpon, Spanish mackerel, and other surf species are cruising both beyond the breakers and inside them, often just a few feet from the sand.

It's important to maintain a retrieve that ensures the plug is swimming at all times; you've got to speed up as an incoming wave begins to push the plug toward the beach, and speed up still more as a wave begins to crash over it, always keeping the line taut, slowing down quickly as the white water passes. It's important to continue swimming the plug until the moment it reaches the sand, because often you'll receive strikes in the thin water just a rod's length from where you're standing.

More than with any other plug, I've enjoyed extraordinary results while fishing a teaser ahead of a Danny surface swimmer. I'm partial to a Clouser saltwater minnow fly with an epoxy head tied on a 2/0 or 3/0 hook. I have, however, used a Lefty's Deceiver, Half and Half, menhaden, and epoxy-head flies and a variety of other patterns as teasers with fine results.

Subsurface Swimmer

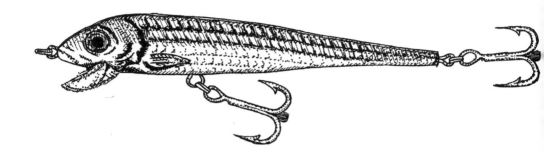

Within the broad category of subsurface swimming plugs are more models and colors than any other plug type. There are dozens of manufacturers and hundreds of different colors, emulating every forage fish a game fish is apt to seek . . . and then some. Yes, there are even pink plugs!

MODELS

The majority of subsurface swimmers are molded of plastic and really don't vary that much from brand to brand. Simply stated, they're designed to dive beneath the surface. The faster you retrieve them, within reason, the deeper they dive. Some even have a larger lip surface to draw them into the depths, while others are weighted. More and more models now have BBs or rattle chambers to emit sounds that are characteristic of baitfish. Among the more popular models are the Bomber, Rapala, Yo-Zuri, Tsunami, and Rebel, to name but a few. Also included in this category are models such as the Creek Chub Pikie Minnow that have a metal lip, which draws them into the depths during the retrieve. All these plugs also produce well with a teaser.

A six-year-old entry into this category is the Stillwater Beachrunner, introduced by Lori and Allen Hoke of Manheim, Pennsylvania. Both are avid surfcasters who fish New Jersey beaches and visit the picturesque beaches of Block Island, Rhode Island. While the couple manufacture a wide array of fine saltwater plugs, their personal favorite is the Beachrunner.

These plugs are available in two sizes, a 7-inch model that weighs 1 ounce and a 5-inch model that weighs 1/2 ounce. They're also available in 15 different colors to closely imitate everything from bay anchovies to menhaden, mullet, herring, and the myriad other forage species found along the coast. Surprisingly, Lori and Allen's favorite color is the yellow shad. I've come to call this the "corncob," because the color closely resembles an ear of corn, and stripers, blues, and weaks attack it with a vengeance.

FISHING THE LURE

The Beachrunner and other subsurface swimmers are most often effective when retrieved slowly, so they're working just beneath the surface. The speed of your retrieve will understandably vary based on surf conditions. The key, however, is to keep slack out of the line. You can actually feel the lure working, or "swimming," as you retrieve it. Avoid at all costs becoming a mechanical caster. It is the single biggest mistake made by so very many surfcasters, who simply cast and retrieve with no regard to lure action, regardless of the lure being used.

While casting the subsurface swimming plug a good distance from the beach often produces strikes from fish holding well offshore, more often than not you'll receive strikes within a couple of rod lengths of where you're standing. Toward this end, be certain to lower your rod tip as the lure works in close and literally swim it onto the sand.

Mirror Plug

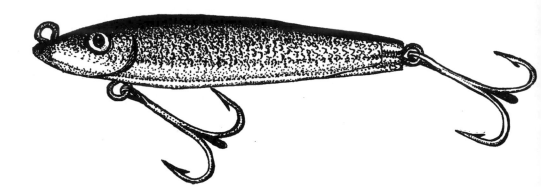

I coined the term *mirror plug* at a time when it was inappropriate to use trade names in magazine articles. This was shortly after Harold LeMaster created the MirrOlure plug, with his unique use of a mirror to create a flashing lifelike appearance. The plugs, developed in his Florida shop, saw instant acceptance from anglers who caught a wide variety of species on them from boats and along the Sunshine State's many miles of surf, where tarpon, snook, sea trout, ladyfish, jacks, and blue runners assaulted it. My first experience with it occurred during our Florida honeymoon while casting from the pristine beaches of Miami Beach, where I caught jacks until arm-weary.

Shortly thereafter Harold and I communicated, and he persuaded me to give the MirrOlure a try as I climbed around coastal jetties and roamed the beaches. I immediately began scoring with stripers and weakfish.

FISHING THE LURE

The MirrOlure is a twitch bait in that it has the profile of a small fish, but doesn't have a lip as do many subsurface plugs. Instead it features an eye on the top of the head to which the leader or snap is attached. When retrieved steadily the MirrOlure doesn't have the customary side-to-side swimming action of most plugs. It has a tendency to slip and slide enticingly. Its action can be enhanced with slight twitches of your rod tip, causing it to dart from side to side, mimicking a wounded baitfish.

The unweighted 52M MirrOlure in 1/2-ounce size has a sink rate of 1 foot per second. Be aware that if you immediately begin your retrieve when the lure hits the water, you'll be retrieving it in the upper stratum of the water column, while the fish may be feeding 6 to 10 feet beneath this level. Thus it's important to hesitate and permit the lure to get well into the depths. That's where you'll usually receive strikes, especially from species prowling the bottom along the surf line in search of a meal.

I've enjoyed excellent results with weighted MirrOlures such as the 77M and 85M. These weigh 1 1/4 and 2 ounces, respectively, and as a result of their shape and weight cast extremely well in a strong onshore wind—a characteristic that's lacking in many plugs. Their fast sink rate is a plus in a heavy surf, as in a northeaster, for they get down in the water column.

I've had especially fine results with the 77M and 85M in deep, swift inlet waters. Cast up and across the current, the plug sinks much like a leadhead jig, and the current sweeps it along through the depths, especially on an ebbing tide, where hungry game fish are waiting for a meal. I've scored on stripers, blues, and weaks throughout the Northeast using this technique, as well as on snook, tarpon, and sea trout in Sebastian Inlet and Government Cut in Florida.

Bottle Plug

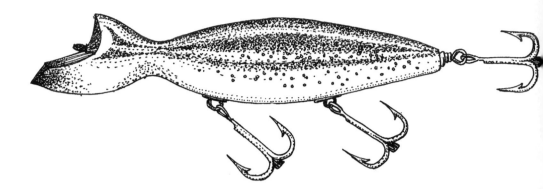

The name *bottle plug* conjures up images of a bottle—a rather unglamorous name for a plug. How the name was coined remains a mystery, except perhaps that its posterior resembles a bottle. Its head is something else again, and it's the head that makes this plug work remarkably well.

The head of the wooden plug is cut in a circular and concave manner, resulting in the lower portion of jaw of the plug forming a lip that extends farther forward than the cut on the top. Because of this design, and lacking a metal lip that causes wind resistance, the bottle plug casts with minimal wind resistance.

In recent years, with the advent of braided lines, anglers have been able to extend their casts by 100 feet or more. By using a bottle plug, many anglers can cast even farther, with the end result that the plug can be put within range of greater numbers of feeding fish than ever before. There are many spots, such as tide rips, rocky bottoms, and drop-offs, that were previously beyond range but are now possible thanks to the design of this versatile plug.

I've found the bottle plug to be a delight to use, especially the wooden models like those made by Dan Smalley of Gibbs Lures. When the plug plummets in at the end of the cast, its design pulls it under as the retrieve is begun. It's a very forgiving style. The plug dives deep during your retrieve, and it will dig deeper still if you speed up; even if you slow down, it will continue to wobble enticingly and draw strikes.

It covers the entire water column, depending on your retrieve speed, which makes it especially effective when you want to probe the depths, especially where there's a sheer drop-off from the beach.

As with most plugs, the bottle plug is available in a wide variety of colors. Some are meticulously painted to simulate bunker, herring, or mackerel, while others are simply pure white or jet black. Some theorize that dark colors produce best at night. I believe it's the action of the plug that makes the difference, with the color a secondary consideration.

Over the past several years we've seen a tremendous influx of baby weakfish in coastal bays and rivers along the Middle and North Atlantic coast. When these weakfish fry vacate the protected inshore reaches in the fall, they become fair game for stripers, blues, fluke, and other surf species. At such times I've been partial to using a yellow flash bottle plug, because its color approximates that of a weakfish. I've enjoyed fine results.

Shore-based river fishermen regularly employ these big plugs, which measure up to 8 inches in length. Bottle plugs allow you to wade the shallows that are typical of many riverbanks, yet still reach the channels well out from shore.

Popping Plug

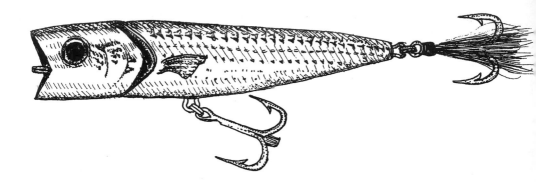

Of all the plug types in the arsenal of surfcasters, the popping plug is among the most popular, because it brings exciting surface strikes from a wide variety of game fish. A simple plug by design, it floats and has a cigarlike shape with a concave head. Most are one piece, but several manufacturers have developed two-piece models that have gained popularity.

FISHING THE LURE

With a popping plug you've got to work your rod tip to impart action. It takes a disciplined effort to retrieve, all the while working your rod tip. The action imparted by the rod tip pushes water ahead of the plug's concave head, causing a surface disturbance not unlike that of a frightened baitfish fluttering about on the surface.

With the two-piece models not only does the plug push water ahead of it, but there's also an enticing side-to-side wiggle. This combination, with a rattle inside the plug that emits a sound of much the same frequency as injured or panicked baitfish, brings exciting strikes.

There's no guarantee, however, and varying the retrieve is often key to success. Perhaps the single biggest mistake anglers make is to retrieve a popping plug too fast at a steady speed. Often a gentle pop, with a hesitation, accompanied by another pop, will result in a exciting surface strike.

Sometimes tarpon, snook, stripers, blues, and weakfish will swirl behind a popping plug, often coming within inches of striking yet veering away at the last instant. I've observed stripers make as many as 8 or 10 passes. When this happens, immediately try a different retrieve on your next cast—either faster or slower—while varying the tip action to excite the wary fish to strike.

Because the popping plug is a surface lure, you can fish it in spots where you'd be apt to hang up if you used a subsurface lure. This is particularly true where there's a lot of boulder-strewn bottom off a stretch of beach, or a natural rock outcropping. I've found it especially effective to work a popper over the submerged rocks of jetties where the ocean has tumbled many of the rocks in a mushroomlike pattern at the end of the jetty. Often game fish lurk in among the rocks searching for a meal.

MODELS

Popping plugs come in a wide range of sizes, from $1/2$-ounce models on up to 3 ounces and more, with almost every color combination in the rainbow. I've found that the surface disturbance made by a popper is the key to success, rather than the color—all the fish really get to see is the plug's white underbelly.

Rattle Plug

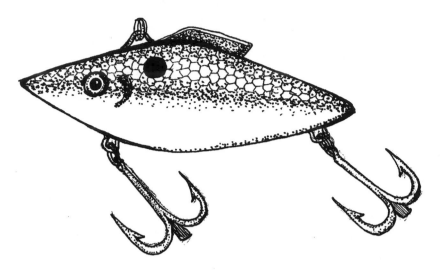

Within the broad assortment of plugs available to surf fishermen are increasing numbers that have some sort of a rattle or noise mechanism within them. These include some of the popper, surface and subsurface swimmer, darter, pencil popper, and other plugs. However, the plug that in my view began the rattle plug revolution is the famous Rat-L-Trap, manufactured by Bill Lewis Lures.

The company takes great care to manufacture rattle chambers whose natural-seeming sounds are nearly identical to those made by schooling shad under distress. They've gone so far as to have an independent analysis done by Cetacean Research Technology of Seattle, Washington, which showed a strong correlation in the frequency domains of the two sounds. According to Joe Olson, Cetacean's president, the spectra from both the schooling shad and the Rat-L-Trap are nearly identical. The sounds emitted by the rattle chamber are highly effective in attracting game fish and stimulating aggressive feeding behavior.

Taking it a step farther, the Rat-L-Trap's shad shape is very similar to the forage on which surf species feed. Baby menhaden, butterfish, blueback herring, hickory shad, and bay anchovies have a very similar profile. Adding still another dimension is the availability of more than 100 colors, many of which closely resemble the afore-mentioned forage. The plug's newest feature is a "bleeding shad," or red coloration around the gill area and bloodred Kahle treble hooks from Eagle Claw.

The plug has a tail and belly treble hook. The eye for attaching a leader snap is located on top of the plug's head, just forward of a tapered dorsal fin that flows across its back. As it's retrieved, the plug moves along head-down, vibrating violently.

FISHING THE LURE

While fishing the surf I've most often used the $1/2$- or 1-ounce models, which measure 3 inches in length, although I'm not averse to using the 1 $1/2$-ounce model that measures 4 $1/2$ inches, especially when there's an onshore wind and big baitfish in the area and I need to add casting distance.

The Rat-L-Trap plug, and many similar-style plugs made by other companies, has a very pronounced action as you retrieve it. You can actually feel it vibrating. It results in the most violent strikes of any plug I've ever used. They're made in surface models, but I've enjoyed best results with the sinking model.

I've scored with the Rat-L-Trap the length of the Atlantic coast while fishing from the surf, scoring on stripers, blues, weaks, fluke, spotted weakfish, redfish, snook, jacks, and barracuda—which says a lot for this hot lure.

Darter Plug

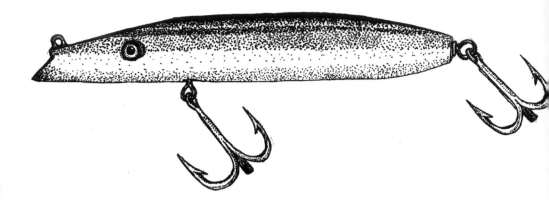

At first glance the Darter plug looks like the most basic of plug designs. It has a round, elongated tapered body, with an angled cut into the face of the plug. Plain and simple, but it does catch fish, and it's a longtime favorite of casters the length of the Atlantic.

MODELS

I began using Darters many years ago when Harry Heinzerling was running things at Creek Chub Bait Company. The Pikie Minnow swimming plugs were long a favorite of mine, and Harry persuaded me to try some of their new Darter models in saltwater sizes, because their freshwater models had a great reputation among largemouth and northern pike devotees.

My favorites included the blue flash, silver flash, and yellow flash finishes, which worked extremely well with big blues and stripers, and from that point forward I became a believer in the Darter.

FISHING THE LURE

Fast-forward to the era of plastics and introduction to the Super Strike Zig Zag turned out by Steve Musso and the staff at his Farmingdale, Long Island, plant. The spot was Shagwong Point, among one of the finest surfcasting locations on the East Coast. I was fishing with Tom Melton, *Fisherman* magazine editor, who persuaded me to put on a "real plug," which turned out to be the Zig Zag. Joining us was Al Ristori, a fellow outdoor scribe with whom I've fished at many of the East Coast's hot spots.

It was one of those autumn nights when it felt good wearing waders to ward off the onshore wind and waves buffeting us. On my first cast I immediately knew I'd like the Zig Zag, for its profile cast like a bullet, with a low trajectory into the wind. As I began the retrieve, the plug immediately lived up to its name, for it zigzagged with abandon, with a steady vibration on the rod tip. The ebbing tide formed a churning rip about 150 feet from the beach, and we could see bunker and other forage struggling on the surface.

It took but a few casts before what walloped the Zig Zag felt like a ton of bricks—a husky bluefish. The combination of an onshore wind, rough surf, screaming current, and big bluefish tested our angling mettle. The lower the tide got, the more hectic the action.

On subsequent trips to Shangwong Point the Zig Zag produced husky stripers. The 2 3/8-ounce darter, measuring 6 5/8 inches in length, proved equally effective in the strong rip under the Lighthouse, Jones Reef, and North Bar.

The key is keeping the line taut and permitting a lateral current along the beach to help maintain its zigzag action. Vary the speed of your retrieve until you hit the right combination, while twitching your rod tip to enhance the darter's action.

Pencil Popper Plug

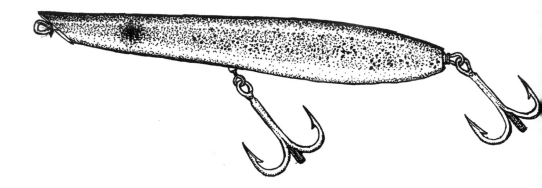

If my memory is correct, the first time I used a pencil popper was while fishing with Stan Gibbs. Buzzards Bay, Massachusetts, was the locale, and huge bluefish were the target. Stan lived on the banks of the Cape Cod Canal, where he turned his wooden plugs on a lathe and trailered his outboard-powered skiff to wherever the action was hottest.

Stan was a perfectionist when making plugs, and when you fished with him you immediately became aware that he had a magical touch, which resulted in his plugs working like no other. It showed in the catch rate, for when I fished with this veteran, his wooden creations produced.

The pencil popper has all of its bulk concentrated in its tail, to which some manufacturers even add weight internally. The plug is then tapered to a very thin head—for a popper, there's a very tiny popping surface in relation to the size of the plug. The head has a slightly concave configuration that pushes water ahead as it's retrieved.

Pencil poppers come in a wide range of colors, but I firmly believe it's the action that catches the fish, with the finish catching the fisherman. Again, all that the fish really see as a popper is dancing on the surface is its predominantly white underbelly.

They're made in sizes ranging from 3-inch models weighing 1/2 ounce—great for weakfish and small blues—on up to 8-inch beauties that weigh 3 ounces and can be cast a country mile with ease. Wood or plastic, the choice is yours. I've used both with fine results. Wood gives you memories, as nothing is more satisfying than digging in your surf bag and snapping on the tooth-riddled, finish-destroyed favorite that has brought you countless fine catches. The plastic looks new virtually forever.

FISHING THE LURE

Stan Gibbs always felt the most effective retrieve was to point the rod tip at the plug and induce a rapid up-and-down tip action. Watching a veteran make a pencil popper work is a thing of beauty. The plug dances from side to side on the surface in an enticing manner, not unlike that of a struggling baitfish. Often in my lagoon in Mantoloking I've watched menhaden, herring, and other forage fluttering on the surface, and the pencil popper closely replicates this distressed movement.

While some plugs and other lures work best with a fast retrieve, slow down with the pencil popper. Its fish-catching effectiveness comes with the action you impart to the plug, and slower is usually better than faster.

Many surfcasters who enjoy fishing a pencil popper choose a rod with a "whippy" action, finding that the soft tip gives just enough of the tantalizing side-to-side motion that makes the plug so effective.

Bullet Plug

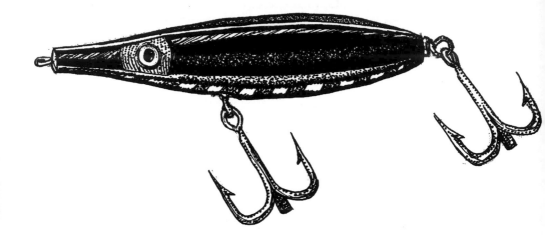

By its very name, you know that the bullet plug is designed to travel like a bullet, directly to its target. So many plugs, irrespective of their weight, are difficult to cast as a result of their aerodynamic design. The bullet plug has castability as a result of its long, tapered shape, with the bulk of its diameter and weight toward the rear.

Sink it does, for the plug, which really has many of the characteristics of a needlefish plug, is designed not only to cast well when there's an onshore wind, but also to probe the depths.

How many times have you been on the beach with a northeaster howling, and the surf is turned to white by cresting and crashing waves, wind blowing spray from the wave tops, and you just can't seem to put a plug where you want it? A bullet plug may be what you need.

MODELS

There are several variations on this basic plug design on the market, most ranging from 1 1/2 to 2 1/2 ounces in weight, and in length from 4 1/2 to 6 inches. What does the plug resemble? It has the profile of most small forage species, such as mullet, peanut bunker, herring, and hickory shad. Color is a matter of choice, to approximate the baitfish in residence.

FISHING THE LURE

The key in fishing a bullet plug is taking advantage of its design, which in rough-water conditions does two things: Its shape results in a respectable cast, and its weight gets it deep in the water column.

With an onshore wind you'll often have a strong current running parallel to the beach. Standing in one spot and mechanically casting and retrieving is usually the least productive method of fishing heavy surf. After determining the direction of the current, cast up into it at a 20- or 30-degree angle. Cast at the horizon line, because this keeps the trajectory of the bullet plug low and to the target—an important consideration with wind.

When the plug hits the water, immediately take up any slack so you have control and the line isn't being tumbled about. Hesitate before you begin your retrieve. This enables the plug to settle into the water column, which is where hungry game fish are most often feeding in heavy weather.

As the current begins to sweep the plug along, begin a slow retrieve, twitching your rod tip occasionally, making the plug react much like a struggling forage fish. Slowly walk in the direction the current is moving your plug; this will prevent the current from causing drag on the line, which would push the plug toward the surface. Continue walking until your retrieve is complete. Ideally, the current will not have carried the plug beyond where you're walking, working all the way to the beach with little drag. I'll often walk a mile or two, just probing the rough surf, and walk into pods of feeding weakfish, stripers, blues, and even fluke.

Little Neck Popping Plug

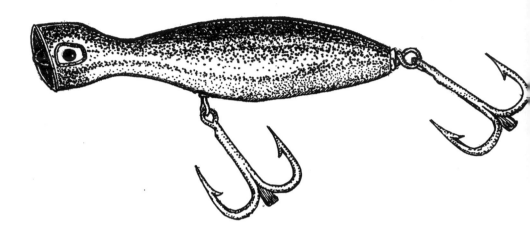

Interchangeably called a Little Neck Popper and a Polaris Popper, this is a cute little plug having a shape not unlike a serpent, with a big concave head tapering to a very thin neck and a bulky body continuing to the tail. Add in the big eyes painted on the head, and you've got a mini Loch Ness Monster!

MODELS

This plug's design, with the weight concentrated toward the tail, enables you to cast it with ease—a major consideration when fishing from the beach. Available in sizes ranging from 1/2 ounce through 3 ounces, and in lengths from 3 to 8 inches, some with a bucktail skirt, it's a plug that you can lean into and comfortably cast a good distance even into an onshore wind.

As I write this I can vividly recall exciting strikes received from a wide variety of game fish. Most notably, in the half-light of dawn, just before the sun peeks over the horizon—my favorite time to fish—I've seen huge tarpon roll behind the plug, leaving a boil the size of a trash can, only to come back, mouths agape, and inhale the offering as they headed skyward. Talk about an adrenaline rush!

My memories are etched with similar experiences that occurred with bluefish, snook, stripers, weakfish, redfish, and jacks, all exciting surface strikes. Some were just a subtle inhaling of the plug, others vicious strikes as though it were the last food in the sea.

FISHING THE LURE

The Little Neck's unique head and neck configuration give you the opportunity to fish it differently from other popping plugs. It floats at rest on the surface, and should be retrieved ever so slowly, with slight twitches of the rod tip causing the concave head to push water ahead of it in a gurgling, splashing movement. It's this movement, and the accompanying sound that carries into the depths, that attracts cruising game fish searching for a meal—the plug appears as a forage species in distress.

Its most unique feature is that it can be retrieved much like a swimming plug. Slowly retrieved, the water flows into the concave head, causing the plug to produce a side-to-side swimming action as the water is pushed out of the head and flows back across its thin neck.

Slowly swimming it, with intermittent twitches of the rod tip, gives the Little Neck an enticing action. You can even let the plug rest motionless for a moment, and then impart just enough tip action to cause it to pop and gurgle. Vary the speed and make it irresistible.

The Little Neck will bring you exciting strikes, to be sure. But make certain not to becoming mechanical in nature when retrieving.

Needlefish Plug

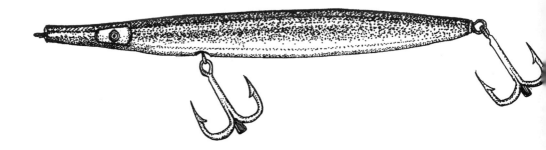

N eedlefish aren't often thought of as a prime bait for surf species. In fact, many anglers don't even realize that needlefish are swimming just beyond the breakers.

The needlefish found in salt water closely resembles the freshwater gar. Its jaw is long and thin, with rows of sharp, needlelike teeth— hence the name. The body color ranges from blue to green on the back, with white sides and bottom that often take on a silver color.

You'll observe needlefish just a few inches in length that are almost transparent, yet it's not unusual to observe 12-inch specimens.

MODELS

The development of the needlefish plug was evolutionary. From my observation as I've traveled along the coast, the majority were turned out in basement workshops by anglers for their personal use. Years ago Stan Gibbs added a needlefish plug to his line of fine wooden plugs, and it's still being produced. Made in 1 3/4-ounce size, it has a long, thin profile, with the head of the plug tapered very thin for approximately a quarter of its length.

Another fine needlefish plug is the Super "N" Fish that was developed by Steve Musso of Super Strike Lures in Farmingdale, Long Island. Steve's needlefish plug has an aerodynamic design, tapered fore and aft, that enables it to be cast into an onshore wind with ease. It's available in a variety of colors that simulate the colors of a needlefish, with a 5 1/4-inch, 3/4-ounce floating model very popular. Three sinking models range from 1 to 1 3/4 ounces in weight, and up to 7 1/4 inches in length.

FISHING THE LURE

Unlike popping plugs, which for the most part are worked with a vigorous tip action, the needlefish entices strikes by subtly sliding through the water with very little surface disturbance. Veteran surf anglers enhance the action by altering the speed of retrieve, twitching the rod tip ever so slightly, much like a needlefish basking in the sun just beneath the surface. The needlefish is especially effective when sand eels invade the surf.

Colors such as black, black and neon orange, smoky, and transparent amber are favored, because they closely resemble the dark coloration of sand eels. The sinking models should always be permitted to settle to the bottom before you begin your retrieve when sand eels are the predominant baitfish. By reeling too soon, the plug will be too high in the water column, far above where hungry game fish are foraging for sand eels slithering in the sand.

Many anglers add a 1-ounce trolling sinker between line and leader when using a floating needlefish plug, which helps take it deep and permits it to swim along just a foot or two off the bottom. The popular needlefish plug regularly attracts strikes from a multitude of surf species, including redfish, tarpon, snook, stripers, bluefish, and weakfish.

Hammered Stainless-Steel Jig

There are a variety of stainless-steel jigs on the market today, but when I think of a hammered stainless-steel jig it always brings memories of the famed Hopkins line of jigs. Years ago it was editorially inappropriate to use the trade name of a lure in magazine articles, so while writing for Frank Woolner, editor of *Salt Water Sportsman,* I referred to a Hopkins No-Eql or Shorty as a "hammered stainless-steel jig." At the time Hopkins had a patent on the lure, and its creator even asked me to verify its unique characteristics as he battled those who would infringe on his patent. Today there are many copies, but none can match the quality of the original. Indeed, unless you lose it as a result of a line break, it's a lure that will last a lifetime, despite the corrosive salt environment in which it's used.

MODELS

The No-Eql is long and rather narrow, while the Shorty is short and stubby. The front and rear of both lures are slightly concave and smooth, while the center looks as though it's been hammered with a ball peen hammer. A stainless-steel split ring is attached to the tail of the lure, to which the hook is attached. To this day the majority of the Hopkins lures are sold with a treble hook. While this hooks more fish, it also makes hook removal difficult, especially for fish about to be released.

I much prefer to use models with a single O'Shaughnessy hook, dressed with either a tuft of feathers or bucktail, or a soft plastic tube. White bucktail is favored, although for the tube tail colors such as green, white, red, or purple prove effective. The lures are available as light as $1/4$ ounce and range up to high-surf models weighing 4 ounces. My time-honored favorite is just plain vanilla, stainless steel all the way. Some models are gold plated. Others have Mylar and fluorescent striping for appeal.

FISHING THE LURE

The key to using these lures from the surf and jetties is maintaining a retrieve speed that permits them to swim enticingly from side to side. You've got to be alert and vary your retrieve speed depending upon the action of the waves. These are also good jigging lures from boats.

Of the many lure types available to the surfcaster, the Hopkins No-Eql and Shorty are among the best casting lures, especially effective when an onshore wind or stiff northeaster is causing wild surf. The No-Eql, being long and thin, is ideal when sand eels or spearing are the prevailing baitfish. The Shorty fits the bill when menhaden or mullet are plentiful. Not only do these lures achieve greater distance than bulkier plugs and leadheads, but they can also be worked deep in the water column. At the completion of a cast, especially when it's rough, permit the lure to settle for a couple of seconds and you'll get it down to where fish are feeding near the bottom.

Block Tin Squids

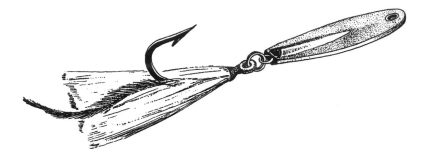

When I began surf fishing, the "standard" lure used by the beach fraternity was the block tin squid. With the passage of time, plugs, leadheads, and a wide variety of other metal lures came into vogue. But to this day the block tin squid has its devotees, who consistently catch a wide variety of species on this versatile lure.

MODELS

As its name implies, the block tin squid is molded of tin. The primary appeal of block tin in making a fishing lure is the ease with which it can be molded, but more important are its soft luster and a silvery color that doesn't tarnish in salt water, as do lures made of lead.

Over the years there have been thousands of models of block tin squids developed, by far the majority meticulously crafted in home workshops. As a teenager I regularly modified existing tin squid models. I then fashioned a mold of dental plaster, which I cured on top

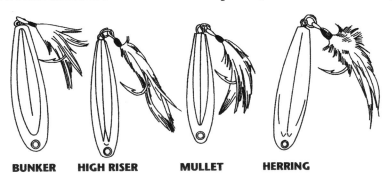

BUNKER   HIGH RISER   MULLET   HERRING

of a coal furnace in our basement. This removed all the moisture from the mold, after which I could pour in molten tin and make lures.

In the early days tin squids had a single 7/0 or 8/0 O'Shaughnessy hook molded into them. A strip of pork rind was draped on the hook, or some anglers would meticulously tie feathers to the tail of the squid. With the passage of time, anglers realized that a free-swinging hook worked better: As the cast was executed the hook, with a feather or bucktail skirt, would lie back over the lure, offering less wind resistance and a longer cast.

Each creator of a style of tin squid gives it a name, including such popular models as the sand eel, which is long and thin, or the mullet, which is short and stubby. There are models made to simulate every baitfish, from the fat butterfish to the spearing, bunker, and others. Without question the broadest selection of pure tins are those created by Charlie Graves, who hailed from Long Island. Now made by West End Fishing Tackle, the tins catch a wide variety of species. When they tarnish after repeated use, touching up with a steel-wool pad restores their luster.

FISHING THE LURE

The keel of the tin squid gives it an enticing side-to-side swimming action during its retrieve. While with some lures an erratic retrieve works best, with tin squids I've found that a steady retrieve, maintaining lure control at all times, is the key. As a wave pushes your lure toward the beach, it's important to speed up your retrieve; slow down when the wave recedes, keeping the tin swimming at all times.

However, it's important not to become a mechanical caster. Varying your retrieve is especially important on a beach with a sheer drop-off, where you should execute your cast, and then permit the jig to settle into the water column before beginning your retrieve.

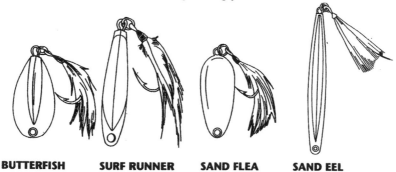

BUTTERFISH   **SURF RUNNER**   **SAND FLEA**   **SAND EEL**

Rigged Eel

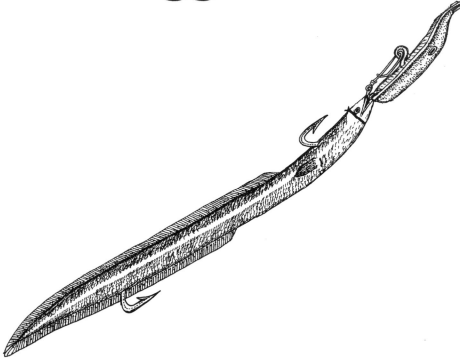

When is a bait a lure, or vice versa? Either way, it happens when you combine a natural bait, such as the American eel, with a block tin squid expressly designed for rigging eels. While it's a natural bait, the American eel when rigged is fished much like a plug or other lure. The rigged eel has long been a favorite of striped bass fishermen, but also accounts for bluefish—which bite it to pieces as they strike—along with weakfish, fluke, cobia, and channel bass.

American eels are a popular live bait and easily obtained at most coastal tackle shops. Those anglers who prefer to rig their eels usually purchase them live. They then make a strong brine solution of coarse salt and water, and place the eels in the brine. This kills the eel, at which time it expunges the contents of its stomach. By leaving the eels in the brine solution overnight, it hardens them. Remove them, wash the slime from them in cold water, and they're ready to rig.

RIGGING THE EEL

For rigging you'll require a block tin eel rig squid, 50-pound-test Dacron rigging line, a 6/0, 7/0, or 8/0 O'Shaughnessy hook, dental floss or rigging twine, and a rigging needle. I'll usually rig six or eight eels at a time, ranging in length from 8 to 18 inches.

Lay the eel flat and run the rigging needle into its mouth and through the stomach; have it exit just behind the vent. Slip a looped piece of Dacron rigging line onto the open loop of the rigging needle and pull it through the eel, exiting behind the vent. Next, slip an O'Shaughnessy hook, of a size appropriate for the eel being used, onto the looped Dacron, and pull the hook gently into the eel, so that it lies flat.

Now run the hook of the eel rig squid in the lower jaw of the eel and out through the head, just behind the eyes. Tie off the Dacron rigging line to the hook eye that extends up from the top of the rigging squid. Complete the rigging by using dental floss or rigging twine to tie off just behind the eyes, so the mouth is shut. Many anglers also tie off where the hook exits the head, and again where the other hook exits behind the vent; this helps keep the eel intact after prolonged use.

Rigged eels can be kept in a strong (two parts salt, one part water) coarse salt brine solution for months. I always have half a dozen or more that I store in the refrigerator in a plastic mayo jar that I get from my neighborhood deli.

FISHING THE EEL

The rigged eel is fished much like a subsurface plug. Cast out, letting the rigged eel to settle near the bottom, which is where game fish are most often searching for a meal. Begin a slow, steady retrieve, and the eel rig squid will give an enticing side-to-side swimming action to the eel. When you receive a strike, lift back smartly to set the hook, and hold on!

Diamond Jig

The diamond jig and its close cousins, the Vike and slab jigs, were for years primarily used to jig for mackerel, pollack, and bluefish. Over time many surfcasters began using them from the beach, with fine results, and today they're an accepted item in the lure pouch.

MODELS

The diamond jig is a four-sided jig, tapered at both ends, molded of lead and usually chrome plated. The slab jig is best described as a diamond jig with two of its edges flattened, making it into somewhat of a slab. The Vike jig has the same basic shape as the diamond but with three sides instead of four; it also usually has a slight bend in it, which on the retrieve gives it more of a side-to-side swimming action than the others.

The tail hook is attached to the diamond jig via a split ring. The jigs most often used by surfcasters range from 1/2 ounce through 3 ounces, and carry a single O'Shaughnessy-style hook. Many of these jigs come equipped with treble hooks, which are easily replaced by the single hook to make hook removal and releasing of fish less difficult.

The single hook may be dressed with either a feather or bucktail skirt. Many anglers slip a piece of plastic tube tail onto the hook in red, green, purple, or yellow. Tube tails hold up better than feathers or bucktails when you encounter bluefish or weakfish, whose teeth can play havoc with the flimsier materials.

FISHING THE JIG

The diamond jig is most effective when there is an abundance of sand eels and spearing in the water. Both of these forage species are very plentiful in the surf, and sand eels in particular often hug the bottom, sometimes actually burying themselves in the sand to elude predators. The diamond gets down deep in even the roughest surf, and can be retrieved with a slow, steady action or with a periodic lifting of the rod tip, causing the jig to slip-slide ahead, then falter, much the way a sand eel or other forage moves along the bottom.

When the surf is rough many anglers use the diamond jig or Vike jig because it casts well, especially when there's an onshore wind. It's often used in conjunction with a teaser fished 30 to 36 inches ahead of the jig. The heavy jig carries the small 2/0 or 3/0 Clouser, Deceiver, or other saltwater fly with ease and gets a small offering within range of feeding fish. It's especially effective when bay anchovies (popularly called rainfish) and other tiny fry are schooled up close to the beach.

The jig also works extremely well when used in conjunction with a multi-lured Sabiki rig when there are mackerel, herring, and hickory shad in the surf: It provides the weight needed for both distance casting and getting deep.

Kastmaster

The Kastmaster is a product of Acme Tackle in Providence, Rhode Island, owned by Art and Al Lavalee. They owned Spencer Plating Company, a jewelry polishing business, and applied their expertise to create the Kastmaster as well as a number of other highly effective saltwater spoons and lures.

MODELS

When I first fished the waters of Narragansett Bay with Art, their most popular lure was the Kastmaster, and I suspect that now, two score years later, it's still at the top of their list. It is simplicity personified, in that it appears to be made from a metal rod, sliced on a bias, much as you'd slice salami. There's a hole at one end of the lure, where the hook is attached via a split ring, and another hole at the other end of the lure to which you attach the leader snap.

The Kastmaster is made in several sizes, from 1/2-ounce on up to 2-ounce models, and it's finished in a jewelry-like luster of either polished chrome or gold. The favored hook is a single O'Shaughnessy, balanced in size to the weight of the lure, ranging from 3/0 through 7/0. The hook is dressed with either bucktail or a replacement feathered skirt. Many anglers prefer the models that come equipped with stiff plastic tubing over the hook; these hold up better, especially when bluefish are encountered, and this is certainly an extremely effective lure for choppers.

FISHING THE LURE

Castability is what helps make the Kastmaster so popular with surf-casters, because it's designed in such a way that it offers very little wind resistance during a cast. This feature, coupled with its weight, enables you to retrieve it effectively from right near the surface as it splashes in at the conclusion of a cast, or letting it settle deeply in a heavy surf and working it through the depths of the water column.

Much of what's important with most lures applies equally to the Kastmaster. You've got to be alert to sea conditions and wave action, and be in control of the lure's action at all times, speeding up as a wave pushes it toward the beach then slowing down as a receding wave pulls against it.

Its thin body permits it to slither along effectively in very shallow water inside the bars along the surf, where forage such as sand eels and spearing are often plentiful. The key in your retrieve with the Kastmaster—and most lures, for that matter—is to lower your rod tip as you retrieve so that as the lure approaches the beach, it stays deep and literally swims onto the sand. Many strikes are received at this critical point, just before the lure reaches the sand. If you're reeling with your rod held high, the lure will tend to balloon up from the depths and be above the strike zone.

Chromed Spoons

You don't often see chromed spoons used by surfcasters, yet there are times when they're especially effective for some species, particularly little tunny (called albacore and bonito along some sections of the Atlantic). The same holds true with Spanish mackerel to the south, and even their cousins the Atlantic mackerel that are found to the north. All three species travel in schools and offer exciting sport.

MODELS

Spoons, as their name implies, have a shape not unlike that of a spoon. They're made of flat metal stock, curved to form a spoon shape, and tapered at the head and tail. Some have a fixed O'Shaughnessy-style hooked attached to the spoon with a small nut and bolt. Others have a split ring at the tail, along with a free-swinging hook usually dressed with feathers or bucktail.

Surf sizes range from tiny 1-inch-long shad spoons to 4- and 5-inch-long models up to an inch in width that target larger game species. They are by design very lightweight, and while the heavier models can be cast fairly well if you use a light outfit, many anglers find it beneficial to add a trolling sinker, two or three feet ahead of the spoon, between line and leader, for the extra weight often necessary to execute a long cast.

FISHING THE LURE

A rig I've often employed with spoons consists of using a 1/2- or 1-ounce troller sinker that I position between my line and a 3-foot-long leader. I then attach a spoon like a Fiord or Hopkins to the terminal end of the leader. Rigged in this manner, a spoon can effectively be cast a good distance, and it will work deep in the water column as a result of the sinker, which performs in much the same manner as a trolled spoon. The key is keeping a tight line and steady retrieve, which gives the spoon an enticing side-to-side swimming action.

I've scored with many little tunny and Spanish mackerel using this rig, from Jersey beaches all the way to Florida. While both of these species often shun conventional metal squids, diamond jigs, plugs, and leadheads, the flashing, twisting action of a chromed or gold-plated spoon turns them on.

The tiny chromed shad spoons used by anglers who fish river waters as American shad make their spawning run each spring work equally well along the surf, from jetties, and especially in inlets. I regularly use these tiny 1- and 2-inch-long spoons when tailor bluefish, blueback herring, hickory shad, and small weakfish are in the surf. I've even caught fluke on the small spoons. They work especially well when there are lots of bay anchovies in the area. These small baitfish—often called rainfish or glass minnows, because they're tiny and nearly transparent—are often found along the surf in huge schools. When the fish are feeding on them, they simply won't strike a large lure.

Jetty Caster Leadhead

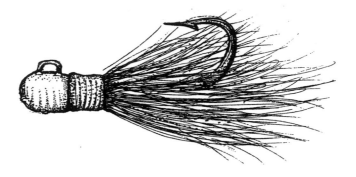

Of the various leadhead jigs available commercially, a particular favorite of mine is the Jetty Caster manufactured by Richie Andrus of Andrus Bucktails. It's unique in several ways. Unlike most leadheads, which use a jighead hook, the Jetty Caster has its hook (a 7/0 O'Shaughnessy) molded into the jig along with a separate eye, which results in the hook extending farther back by 1/2 inch or more. This places the hook farther back into the bucktail skirt, which results in more hookups.

The jig weighs 1 1/2 ounces and because of its shape, much like the nose of an atomic sub, casts like a proverbial bullet with little wind resistance. The full-bodied bucktail skirt is hand-tied, and it's available in white. As with most leadheads, I slip a strip of pork rind onto the hook. This makes the lure a far more effective fish catcher than when fished plain.

FISHING THE JIG

I first used a Jetty Caster leadhead while fishing the boulder-strewn water on the south side of Montauk Light. With a stiff northeaster right in my face, I really had to lean into a cast to achieve distance. The key was following Richie's directions and beginning a prompt retrieve, thus keeping the leadhead high in the water column, above the boulders below. Bass and blues assaulted it with abandon, the choppers reducing the bucktail to shreds.

I later began using it from Jersey jetties, where it proved especially effective when strong onshore winds buffeted the jetty fronts, making it virtually impossible to use plugs (tin squids or other metals would work too high in the water column). I often scored with accurate casts over rocks tumbled about the jetty fronts, because the weight of the leadhead kept it from being pushed about, yet I was able to maintain good lure control in the often violent white water. There are a number of other companies that produce the same shape as the Jetty Caster, and it's a good style to have in your kit.

Still another spot where a Jetty Caster proves effective is from the many inlets scattered along the length of the coast. The most effective technique I've found in fishing swift-flowing inlets on an ebbing tide is to bracket the bottom of the entire inlet using a series of retrieves, beginning with short casts and gradually extending the distance. The secret is to cast up into the current at a 45-degree angle and permit the leadhead to settle to the bottom and bounce seaward, all the while maintaining a taut line so you have control of the lure. At the end of the swing, as the jig lifts off bottom, you'll frequently receive a strike. Often it feels as though you've hung bottom. This technique has produced a wide variety of species for me, from stripers, blues, weaks, and fluke in the Northeast to tarpon, channel bass, snook, and jack crevalle farther south.

Jighead

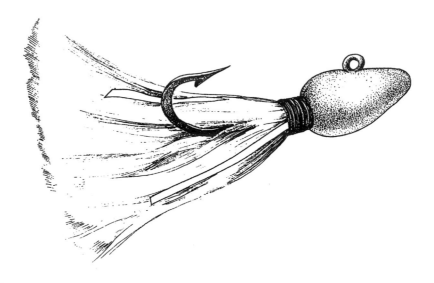

MODELS

The basic jighead is simply a piece of lead molded around an O'Shaughnessy-style jig hook. They're made in sizes ranging from a mere 1/8 ounce up through 6 ounces, although for surf-fishing applications 2 ounces is about as heavy as you'll need. Some models are sold with bucktail skirts, while others are dressed with feathers. Some are plain lead, while others are painted exotic colors to simulate every baitfish imaginable.

The basic jighead is skirtless, and you can select any one of a wide variety of plastic bait tails to simulate the baitfish in residence. As with most lures, it has also evolved into many shapes, including ball, bullet, and torpedo-shaped heads, flatheads, and molded heads that are replicas of forage species, which are airbrushed with minute detail.

What you want to look for when purchasing a jighead is one or two barbs molded into the head around the shank of the hook. This enables you to slide the plastic skirt over the barb, which holds it firmly in place and keeps it from slipping onto the curved J part of the hook.

A unique jighead that I've found to my liking is the Strike King Screw Lock Jighead. Molded into the leadhead of the jig is what looks like a stiff spring, which loosely winds itself around the shank of the hook. Slide a plastic bait tail onto the hook and then turn or screw it around and around, until it snugs firmly to the rear of the jighead. It's made in 1/4-, 3/8-, and 1/2-ounce sizes. I've enjoyed fine results with it for a variety of surf species, including stripers, blues, weaks, and fluke, and never once had a plastic bait tail ripped from the jig, although the blues regularly chop the tails in half. Strike King would do well to offer models in the 1- to 2-ounce size for heavy surf and inlet conditions.

It's also wise to select jigheads that have an O'Shaughnessy hook with an extra-long shank. The hook is then farther back in the plastic bait tail, resulting in fish being hooked that might otherwise have just grabbed the tail end of the bait tail.

FISHING THE JIG

Fishing jigheads from the beach is especially effective when using a lightweight, one-handed spinning or popping outfit. They're great when there's an abundance of forage such as sand eels, spearing, bay anchovies, mullet, and menhaden moving along the surf.

There are several effective techniques, ranging from a slow retrieve to a fast one. A whip retrieve is especially effective, done either fast or slow, by retrieving several feet of line then smartly whipping the rod tip upward. This causes the jig to dart ahead and falter, much like a struggling baitfish. Try the whip retrieve particularly on jacks, Spanish mackerel, blues, snook, weakfish, fluke, and redfish.

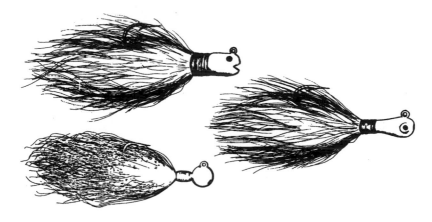

Lima Bean Leadhead

MODELS

Ranging in size from $1/8$ to 2 ounces, the lima-bean-shaped leadhead jig has a long history of catching a wide variety of bottom feeders and game fish from the surf. Its originators were Bill and Morrie Upperman of Atlantic City, New Jersey, who meticulously crafted them in their shop in a loft in the popular resort city. The Upperman Bucktail was, and is, simplicity personified. It's molded of lead with an O'Shaughnessy hook in sizes ranging from 2 through 8/0—the larger the lure, the bigger the hook. There isn't much of a choice with respect to color, either all yellow with a yellow bucktail skirt, or white with a red back and white bucktail skirt.

While the Upperman catches fish just as it comes from the tackle shop, attaching a strip of pork rind to the hook easily enhances its action and fish-catching ability. That strip of pork rind often makes the difference between success and failure, and success has taught me to never use one without a strip of rind.

FISHING THE JIG

There are several retrieval techniques that you can use with the Upperman Bucktail. Cast out and permit the jig to settle to the bottom, then begin your retrieve by sweeping your rod tip upward, causing the bucktail to dart ahead and falter, much like a struggling baitfish. Then continue jigging and retrieving, with the jig continuing to lift off the bottom as though it were darting toward the surface like a struggling sand eel, mullet, or other forage.

The slow, steady retrieve occasionally brings strikes when the whip retrieve draws a blank. When fishing an inlet, a very effective technique is to cast up and across the current, and then permit the Upperman to settle to the bottom. There it will be carried with the current, bouncing along as it goes. Often game fish such as stripers, blues, weakfish, and channel bass will hug the bottom where rips and eddies form on an ebbing tide. As the bucktail lifts off the bottom at the end of its swing, the strike will be received. Frequently it will feel as though you've snagged bottom, because game fish inhale the leadhead leisurely. As you lift back with your rod tip, though, it will be promptly yanked downward, and you're in business.

The Upperman Bucktail and other lima-bean-shaped leadhead jigs are also very effective when slowly jigged along the bottom where summer flounder reside. The flatfish are often right in the curl of the breakers, where they're searching for a meal of sand fleas or crabs, many of which approximate the size of the leadhead. The tumbling action of the waves often exposes the forage, and jigging your bucktail just off the bottom quickly brings strikes. You'll also score with such surf and inlet residents as snook, redfish, blues, tarpon, snappers, and groupers.

Plastic Bait Tail

The first leadhead jigs were often dressed with bucktail or feather skirts, and then adorned with a strip of pork rind. With the advent of soft plastics, the leadhead jig with a plastic bait tail came into being. Al Reinfelder and Lou Palma, more than any other anglers I know, were instrumental in developing and popularizing the bait tail back in 1960. They improved upon the bucktail jig made of lead and bucktail by replacing the body and tail, which was composed of soft plastic; they called the result the Alou Bait Tail jig. The shape of the tail simulates the outline of a typical baitfish, and originally it was available in half a dozen colors: white, pale blue, black, red, orange, and transparent.

I was among the fortunate few who received a handful of their first production from Long Island. We were all young striper fanatics at the time, and shared our ideas and techniques.

From that small beginning the lure type grew in popularity to the point that hardly a surf fisherman ventures onto the beach without adorning a few of the leadheads in his surf bag with soft plastic bait tails. Given today's technology, the plastic bait tails are often exacting replicas of the forage species contiguous to an area, be they sand eels, baby bunker, rainfish, mackerel, herring, mullet, spearing, or any of myriad other baitfish.

All bait tails are not created equal, however. Therein lies their increased popularity in recent years. What were once relatively flat pieces of plastic now have twisted tails that slither enticingly through the water when retrieved. Others have scent built into the plastic, which proves attractive to marauding game fish.

The last several fall seasons have seen huge migrations of baby menhaden from coastal rivers and bays. Popularly called "peanut bunker," literally millions of these 3- to 4-inch-long baitfish move close to the beach as they migrate to the Chesapeake Bay.

Bruce Brown, who heads up Storm Lures, has found it almost impossible to provide tackle shops with an adequate supply of the Storm Wild Eye Swim Shad, which closely resembles the peanut bunker. It has a molded lead body within the soft plastic body with a tail that gives it an enticing action. Wherever you see a breaking striped bass, bluefish, or weakfish and can place a Wild Eye Swim Shad within a few feet of the break, you're hooked up in an instant.

The teeth of weakfish and blues quickly exact attrition on the soft plastic, so it always pays to carry a good backup supply. The lure works well using a steady retrieve, because its tail flutters enticingly, although I've caught many fish while using a whip retrieve, causing the jig to dart ahead and falter much like a struggling baitfish.

I'll often fish a teaser ahead of soft plastic baits, with fine results.

Plastic Shrimp and Crab Jigs

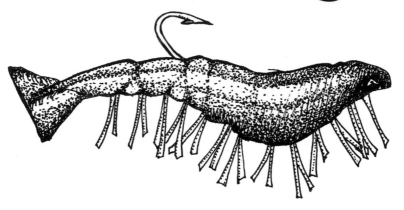

A mong the major forage species found along the surf are shrimp, crabs, and sand bugs. I doubt whether there's a game species along the Atlantic coast surf that hasn't regularly dined on these crustaceans. Indeed, I've removed many from the stomachs of fish that were already crammed so full, I wondered how they expected to get another one in!

While the natural baits of the aforementioned species are regularly used, increasing numbers of surfcasters are turning to shrimp- and crab-shaped soft plastic replicas to entice strikes from hungry game fish and bottom feeders.

MODELS

The soft plastic shrimp and crabs manufactured by D.O.A. Fishing Lures are virtually perfect imitations of the live bait. Their uniqueness lies in the fact the soft plastic body can be filled with real shrimp or a piece of crab, which gives off scent. Often the scent makes the difference between a hungry game fish inhaling the lures and turning away at the last moment.

There are a variety of sizes of shrimp, ranging from 2-inchers that resemble the small grass shrimp found in coastal bays, to 3-, 4-, and 6-inch sizes that resemble the large shrimp of ocean waters. The shrimp are available in a variety of colors as well, with some manufacturers offering more than 36 different color combinations to suit the whims of fish and fishermen. Indeed, while a shrimp is a shrimp, when it comes to plastic shrimp certain colors produce better than others. Some of the colors are exotic, including hot pink, blaze orange, and jet black, while others are in keeping with what you'd expect from a shrimp—pale brown, chartreuse, blue, and green.

Soft plastic crabs are most effective in small sizes, with the 2-inch model ideal. I suspect the small size not only resembles a crab to fish foraging in the surf, but also closely mimics the myriad sand bugs that are constantly churned up and exposed by the waves.

FISHING THE JIGS

In using the shrimp and crab imitations, keep in mind that these forage species do not swim like baitfish. Instead they dart and falter, and sometimes appear to hang suspended in the water before moving ahead in their irreguar pattern. Thus it behooves you to work the lure such that it closely resembles the pattern of the real thing.

Cast out and permit the shrimp or crab to settle to the bottom, then begin your retrieve with a twitching of the rod tip, followed by a slow, irregular retrieve. This lazy, erratic action will often arouse the interest of a game fish or bottom feeder cruising along the surf line as it searches for a meal. The strike you receive is often innocuous, unlike what happens when a fish strikes a surface plug or fast-moving lure. Instead you may feel as though you've simply snagged bottom, for the fish simply swims up and inhales the enticing morsel.

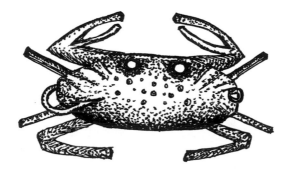

Deceiver Fly

I met the creator of the Deceiver in a rather unusual way many years ago. I was drifting down the Potomac River in a johnboat when an outdoor journalist whose exploits I'd long followed happened by. We drifted along and chatted. Evening was approaching, and the smallmouth bass would soon begin feeding. It was Lefty Kreh who grasped the gunwale and offered me a fly-casting outfit, one of a pair he had on board. I obliged, and marveled at the ease with I could present a deer hair bug to the river's smallmouths.

From that beginning commenced a long friendship. Lefty and I fished everywhere from the mainland to the Bahamas, seeking a wide variety of species on the long rod. It was an era when saltwater fly fishing came into its own. Creative individual that he is, Lefty developed the Deceiver fly, which is tied in many variations. His personal ties of this tuft of bucktail and feathers have been affectionately called the Lefty's Deceiver, and they are must-have patterns in the pouch of every serious fly rodder who plies the surf.

PATTERN VARIATIONS

The Deceiver is perhaps the simplest fly pattern in the caster's arsenal. It's just a tuft of feathers and bucktail tied to a 3/0 hook, with a tiny head and a sprig of red at the gills. The choice of colors includes everything in the rainbow, and at one time or another they will all catch practically every species in the surf. Among the more popular are chartreuse and white when menhaden are present, blue and white when mullet and blueback herring abound, and brown and white when sand lance are the prevailing forage. Some anglers tie all-black Deceivers, while red and yellow have their devotees. It's all a matter of limiting yourself to three or four patterns, with 3/0 size a great all-around choice that will catch everything you're apt to encounter in the surf, from Spanish mackerel to heavyweight stripers.

FISHING THE FLY

The Deceiver can be used effectively with both a floating and a sinking fly line. If you're partial to a sinking line—which generally is best for the majority of surf applications—then you can control the depth of your retrieve by beginning to strip as soon as the fly touches down. This keeps it high in the water column, and is especially effective when mullet or peanut bunker are being herded on the surface.

If the prevailing forage is sand lance, then hesitate and get the Deceiver down deep. This will permit you to snake it along the bottom as you strip-retrieve, much like a sand lance swimming above or preparing to burrow into the sand.

Vary the speed of your retrieve, always attempting to keep slack out of your line so you're in control of the Deceiver. Snake it right onto the sand, too: You'll be surprised at the number of close-to-shore strikes you'll receive.

Crab Fly

The single forage that is available in the surf throughout the season is the crab. These crustaceans scurry about the bottom, taking care of housekeeping chores, consuming any food that's available, including the baits of surf anglers, who view them as pests.

There are many varieties of crabs along the surf, including the blue crab, rock crab, calico crab, and others. While surfcasters often use crabs as bait, anglers armed with spinning or multiplying outfits haven't a lure that replicates a crab, with the exception of the newer crab jigs. Here's where the Crab Fly comes into play. The long-rod devotee can present a fly that represents an hors d'oeuvre to cruising game fish or bottom feeders.

PATTERN VARIATIONS

There are many variations of crab flies to choose from, including the Blue Crab, Merkin Crab, Fleeing Crab, McCrab, Swimming Crab, Raghead Crab, and others. These patterns closely resemble any one of the many crabs found along the surf. In my view they also look much like a sand flea, or sand bug, as they're retrieved.

Toward this end, over a lifetime of fishing the surf I've removed crabs and sand fleas from the stomachs of almost every species I've caught. Stripers, bluefish, weakfish, summer flounder, spot, croaker, and redfish all root along the bottom as they search for a meal, readily inhaling crabs and sand fleas. I've removed upward of two dozen crabs and sand fleas from the stomach of a single fluke. Some were as tiny as my pinkie nail.

FISHING THE FLY

Most fly-rod devotees are accustomed to sight casting the crab fly to bonefish and permit that are cruising shallow tidal flats. In surf fishing, however, you seldom have the opportunity to sight cast. Instead, it's a matter of just walking along a stretch of beach and blind casting.

I must emphasize that with the various fly patterns I've used— most often the Merkin Crab—it's not important to make long casts. When game fish and bottom feeders are searching for crabs and sand fleas, it's usually very close to the sand, where the waves rolling in toward the beach are churning up the bottom and exposing the tasty tidbits.

I usually shoot 40 or 50 feet of line, let it settle to the bottom, and then begin a leisurely two-handed retrieve. The slower you retrieve, the more action you achieve as the fly's legs come to life. Remember that crabs are usually walking along the bottom or leisurely swimming just above it, and the sand fleas are usually right on the bottom, scurrying along.

While catching fish is the ultimate objective with a crab fly, the only time I become upset is when a toothy bluefish grabs the delicate offering. One blue costs me one meticulously tied fly, thanks to its teeth. Other surf species are more accommodating and don't as readily destroy the fly.

Popping Bug

The flies available to the saltwater fly caster are legion. Each season sees more patterns being introduced by the dedicated gentry who spend countless hours at their fly-tying vises designing patterns.

The popping bug that has found such huge popularity among saltwater fly casters is really a takeoff on the same poppers I used for many years while seeking smallmouth and largemouth bass with the long rod. Indeed, I used my favorite freshwater cork-bodied popping bug along the beach while seeking stripers and blues back in 1965. It was exciting to score, but the hooks were bronzed, not tinned, and immediately rusted.

PATTERN VARIATIONS

Fast-forward to today, and we have the creations of many talented fly tiers, including my good friend Bob Popovics. Bob hails from Seaside Park, New Jersey, and created the best saltwater popping bug I've ever used, the Bob's Banger.

It's tied on a long-shank 3/0 or 4/0 stainless-steel hook. The body is made of Styrofoam, approximately 1/2 inch in diameter and 1 inch long. A favorite of mine has the Styrofoam covered with highly reflective silver tape, and a pair of large, self-adhesive eyes. It has a white bucktail skirt, covered with floss where it meets the body of the Styrofoam. Tying instructions are available on Bob Popovics's Web site.

FISHING THE FLY

Big and rather bulky, Bob's Banger isn't as easy to cast as are conventional saltwater flies. On a morning when an offshore breeze has been blowing all night, it's a great popper to probe a stretch of beach during the half-light of dawn. I usually try to be on the beach an hour before first light, just walking and blind casting. At first light, sometimes earlier, the stripers, blues, weaks, and other surf residents begin to boil within a rod's length of the sand, feeding on the tiny fry.

A favorite technique is to use a stripping basket, execute your cast, then tuck the rod under your armpit and employ a two-handed, hand-over-hand retrieve. This gives you total control, popping the fly and causing it to gurgle and splash. Often you'll see fish swirl behind the fly, sometimes half a dozen or more times before they decide to strike.

The key is keeping your rod tip low to the water and standing back on the sand, so you can keep the popping bug working right up until the minute it slides onto the sand. Often the strikes will come in this thin water, which is where the forage species are seeking sanctuary.

Always remember that with the majority of surf species, slower is better. Avoid the bad habit of stripping too fast. Slow and easy will keep the popper gurgling along, with an occasional extra twitch, or even stopping it momentarily. The strikes are electrifying, to put it mildly.

Clouser Minnow Fly

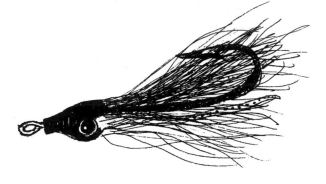

I can say unequivocally that of all the fly patterns I've used in more than four decades of saltwater fly fishing, the Clouser not only is my favorite but has also caught greater numbers of fish, and more species, than any other fly I've used. The Clouser is such a versatile fly that I often go weeks, even months, at a time without ever using anything else. Except, of course, when I stop to retie a fly because of the onslaughts of my briny friends.

PATTERN VARIATIONS

Developed by renowned fly tier Bob Clouser, the Clouser fly has been hailed as the one of the greatest fresh- and saltwater flies ever. The Clouser differs from most flies in that it rides with the hook up. Other flies discussed in this book, like the popping bug, Surf Candy, Deceiver, and crab fly, ride through the water with the hook down.

This is the result of the Clouser having a pair of bead eyes, made of plastic or metal, tied at the head. The eyes are positioned so the weight is beneath the hook, which causes the hook point to ride up during a retrieve. The hook is dressed with bucktail ranging from 2 to 3 inches in length, usually white on the bottom and the color of the prevailing bait on top. Among my favorites are chartreuse and white with silver Mylar, blue and white with silver Mylar, and brown and white with gold Mylar. I prefer Clousers with epoxy heads, which hold up much better.

FISHING THE FLY

I fish the Clouser primarily with a 400-grain sinking fly line and a 6-foot-long 15-pound-test tapered fluorocarbon leader. This combination enables me to cast effortlessly, and believe me when I say you don't normally need 100-foot casts to catch fish on a fly in the surf. Use a stripping basket and stay out of the water, walking on the sand and executing your 40- to 60-foot casts. With your rod tip held low, swim the Clouser onto the sand. Walk a few feet, execute a roll cast then a single backcast, and shoot the fly. Keep working the beach and cover lots of water.

Pay attention to wind when you're casting. The Clouser is the heaviest fly in the saltwater arsenal, and if you're a right-handed caster and the wind is in your face, it can catch the fly line and push both line and fly toward you. Many anglers fail to realize the potential danger and have hooked their neck or ear, so take care.

As you probe the beach, heed the direction the current paralleling the beach is moving. Picture it much as you would a stream, casting up and across the current, and retrieving as the current sweeps parallel to the beach.

The Clouser is my first choice as a teaser, described elsewhere. Its weighted eye holds it away from the primary leader on retrieve, enabling a fish to inhale it with ease. It catches bonus fish when even large fish ignore the primary lure. It literally more than doubles my catch each season.

Surf Candy Fly

The Surf Candy is another fly by Bob Popovics that warrants inclusion in the fly pouch of the long-rod set. It's a departure from most saltwater fly patterns in that it has a head finished in epoxy. Its head has what is best described as a torpedo shape, with body and eyes beneath a hard coating of epoxy and bucktail flowing behind. Its appeal lies in its appearance, which approximates any one of myriad small baitfish found along the surf. Just 3 inches in length, it really isn't a very impressive or fancy pattern.

To a hungry game fish cruising inside a sandbar or along the edge of the drop-off of a steep beach formation, however, the Surf Candy could well be a spearing, bay anchovy, sand lance, or the fry of game fish or bottom feeders. What it does is represent something to eat, and a prowler looking for a meal won't hesitate to wallop it.

FISHING THE FLY

I'll often use an 8-weight outfit with a 400-grain high-density sinking line with a Surf Candy when probing the troughs between sandbars and the beach, or the deep cuts between bars.

As you walk along probing the surf with a Surf Candy, you'll often encounter rock jetties or old wooden groins extending seaward. Forage species like to take up residence among the rocks or along the decaying groins, and you should always take the time to cast parallel to the structures, permitting your fly to settle deep into the water column before beginning your retrieve.

With respect to retrieves, if you're accustomed to casting with one hand and using the other hand to retrieve, coiling your line in a stripping basket, you might try the two-handed, hand-over-hand retrieve. Tuck the rod under your armpit and use both hands to control both the line and the retrieve speed of the fly, which is often impacted by wind or wave action. This eliminates any stop–start action and gives the fly a steady, even retrieve, which you can speed up or slow down, all the while making sure that there's no slack in the line as a result of wave action. You want to have control of the fly's action at all times.

If you're fortunate enough to be fishing the surf where a pond empties into the ocean, or where a river flows seaward, you'll find that casting the Surf Candy can produce with a variety of species. Cast up and across the current on an ebbing tide and permit the line to settle into the depths, all the while being swept seaward as you slowly retrieve. Strikes will often be received at the end of the swing, as the line and Surf Candy lift off the bottom. Often it just feels like you're snagged; then the fish realizes it's hooked and the fun begins!

Menhaden Fly

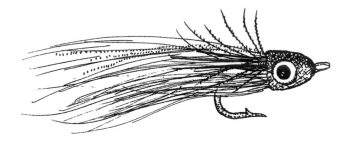

The menhaden is unquestionably one of the most important forage species—if not *the* most important—found on the Atlantic coast. From the time the tiny fry are hatched in bays and estuaries they are a target of the fry of game fish and bottom feeders. When they reach adulthood, the heavyweights that forage along the surf target them.

PATTERN VARIATIONS

A fly tied to resemble a menhaden is essential in the fly pouch of a serious surf fly caster. Menhaden flies—and there are many variations—are basically tied to reflect the bright silvery coloration of this forage species, projecting a high yet narrow profile with large, pronounced eyes. Most menhaden patterns use silver Mylar, which adds a reflective flash that attracts game fish. Keep a wide range of sizes in your fly pouch, from 3- and 4-inch-long patterns designed to resemble peanut bunker on up to those hard-to-cast 6- or 7-inchers that resemble adults.

FISHING THE FLY

As popular as the menhaden fly is, I'm duty-bound to admit that the most productive time to use this pattern is also the time when it's the most frustrating. Menhaden travel in huge schools, often numbering in the tens of thousands and sometimes covering literally acres of water surface. As the schools travel along they can easily be detected, for they flutter about on the surface.

When hungry game fish such as bluefish, stripers, channel bass, and little tunny herd the school and force it to seek sanctuary along the surf, they become fair game for the fly fisherman. The problem rests with the speed at which the schools travel. Often I've waited patiently for a school that's several hundred yards offshore to be herded to the beach, and by quickly executing a cast I've hooked up. By the time I land and release the fish, however, the school has moved either up or down the beach, and often is a quarter mile away. The bunker, pogies, or mossbunker (as menhaden are often called) just keep swimming furiously to evade the onslaughts from below.

Make no mistake, it's exciting fishing. When the menhaden-of-the-year, sometimes called peanut bunker, vacate coastal bays and rivers, they're often traveling in small schools. I like to take up station on a jetty, for as the schools travel along the beach they have to move around the jetty. They're often intercepted by stripers and other game fish, which take up stations in anticipation of the menhaden.

Here, too, it's strenuous fishing, for you get off a cast, hook a fish, land and release it, and have to hustle to get ready for the next school to arrive. In my younger days I'd try to chase after and keep up with the school, but even then it was a virtual impossibility. Toward this end, those who traverse the beaches in beach buggies or four-wheel SUVs are at a decided advantage.

Teaser Rig

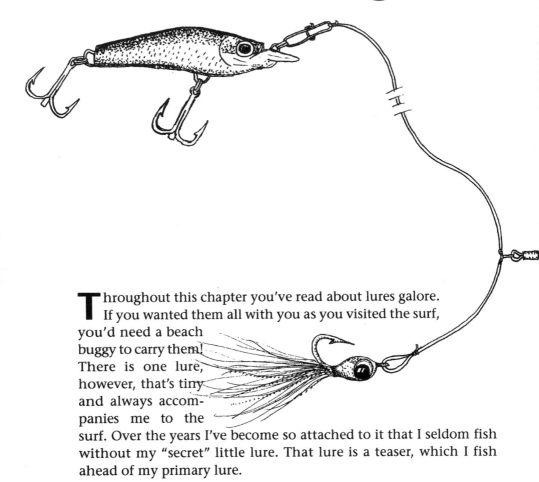

Throughout this chapter you've read about lures galore. If you wanted them all with you as you visited the surf, you'd need a beach buggy to carry them! There is one lure, however, that's tiny and always accompanies me to the surf. Over the years I've become so attached to it that I seldom fish without my "secret" little lure. That lure is a teaser, which I fish ahead of my primary lure.

TYPES OF TEASERS

A teaser can be any one of a variety of small lures, most notably a saltwater fly, a shad dart, a soft plastic bait tail, or just a tuft of feathers or bucktail tied to a hook. It's fished 24 to 48 inches ahead of the primary lure off a dropper loop. Or you can fish the teaser off a long tag end of leader when you tie on your swivel between line and leader. Some anglers simply tie a second, 6- to 10-inch-long piece of leader material to the same swivel that they attach their primary leader to, so it hangs off to the side.

The tiny teaser, fished ahead of a plug, metal squid, or leadhead jig, can resemble any one of many kinds of forage on which fish that frequent the surf feed. I'll often use a Clouser saltwater minnow fly that's tied on a 2/0 or 3/0 hook. It's brown and white with gold Mylar. I catch a lot of fluke on this, many of which have their stomachs filled with tiny sand bugs and crabs. A Lefty's Deceiver fly may resemble a tiny spearing, whereas a large mossbunker fly resembles a peanut bunker. Shad darts and plastic bait tails are good, too.

The Chris's Fly By Night teaser is what I'd call an all-around universal teaser—it's tied to resemble what might be termed a generic baitfish found along the surf. Chris Sauerwein of High Bridge, New Jersey, created the Chris's Fly By Night teaser which is one of the few lures designed expressly as a teaser. You just can't go wrong using one; to a hungry fish searching for a meal, it's a treat that can't be passed up.

In a typical season I catch a wide variety of species on the teaser. Included are striped bass, bluefish, weakfish, fluke, Spanish mackerel, hickory shad, herring, little tunny, channel bass, blue runners, jack crevalle, snook, sea trout, and croaker.

TYING THE TEASER RIG

To tie a leader rigged for a teaser, start with a 4-foot-long piece of 30- or 40-pound-test fluorocarbon leader material. Tie a tiny 50-pound-test Spro power swivel within a dropper loop knot about a foot from one end of the leader material. Pull it rather tight, so the circle of the dropper loop formed is 1/8 to 1/4 inch in diameter. To the short tag end of the leader tie a very small duolock snap, to which the teaser is snapped. Or, if you wish, you can tie on the teaser directly using a perfection knot or uniknot. Complete the leader by tying a medium-sized duolock snap to the terminal end of the leader where you'll be attaching your primary lure, using a uniknot. The barrel swivel on the leader is tied to the terminal end of your line. This puts the teaser approximately 24 to 36 inches ahead of the primary lure. I've even fished the teaser 48 inches ahead of the primary lure, with fine results.

Pork Rind

A long about now you should have a reasonably good under-standing of the large range of lure types most often used by surf and jetty anglers along the Atlantic coast to entice a strike from a hungry game fish. Each of the lures described thus far will catch fish as it comes out of the box. There is, however, a way you can enhance the action of many lures, and that's by adding a strip of pork rind. Yes, an unglamorous piece of pork will often make the difference between success and failure.

I first became a believer in pork rind while fishing from an old bridge spanning the Shrewsbury River in Sea Bright, New Jersey. The bridge tender would let us climb down on the icebreakers, where we'd view stripers, their noses tight to the shadow line formed by the bridge lights. Facing into the current, they'd dart out and grab an unsuspecting spearing struggling against the tide, or a crab being carried along. Often I'd try to entice them to strike a leadhead jig with bucktail skirt, to no avail. An old-timer opined I wasn't catching because I wasn't using a pork rind strip on the leadhead. He offered a strip from a small jar. On the very first cast a feisty striper walloped it as though it were the last meal in the river!

I recount this tale because from that time forward I've carried pork rind and religiously use it on many surf lures. Its use in conjunction with a leadhead jig is almost mandatory. Granted, today's plastic-tailed leadhead jigs have an enticing action of their own. But the traditional leadhead jig with a bucktail or feather skirt will always catch you more fish when it's dressed with a piece of pork rind than when it's fished plain.

Much the same is true with a block tin squid. Some tins come with bucktail skirts, others with feathers, and some have a plain hook. The action of each will be enhanced with the addition of a piece of pork rind.

As far back as I can remember I've been a user of Uncle Josh pork rind. It comes packed in convenient-to-carry small bottles, in a variety of sizes to accommodate each lure. Tailor the strip to the size of the lure you're using. Strips ranging from 2 to 6 inches in overall length are most effective for surf applications with metals and leadheads. White is by far the most popular, although pork rinds in red, blue, yellow, and green are also very popular. Some strips are flat, while others are cut into twisted shapes that enhance their action during the retrieve.

I've also used a pork rind strip with a surface swimming plug with excellent results. The pork rind gives the lure that extra bit of enticing action, whether it's reeled slowly or via a whip retrieve. The whip retrieve, or even just a twitching of the rod tip during the retrieve, is extremely effective with the entire leadhead family, while a slow, steady retrieve proves more productive with tins and swimming plugs.

CHAPTER 6

Natural Baits

The term *natural bait* covers a multitude of forage that surf species feed on. There are other times, however, when the surf is devoid of anything that resembles a meal, and the surf residents are content to feed on almost anything.

Both situations provide excellent opportunities for the shore-based caster. In the former case, if you present a mullet or menhaden on a hook, the game fish is apt to engulf it rather than expend energy chasing a lively fish. In the latter situation, the same fish is just happy to find something to eat.

Throughout this chapter I'll discuss the most popular baits and how to fish them. Many anglers theorize that fresh bait is best, while I've caught many fish on live baits that had expired. While the differences of opinion will continue, I'm of the belief that the key with all natural baits is the presentation, keys to which are detailed in this chapter and throughout this book.

Chunk baits are effective, as are any of the variety of crabs—including rock crabs, calico crabs, and blue crabs—that sometimes carpet the bottom. Whole squid, strips of squid, and squid heads all make fine hook baits. I doubt if there's a sea worm, be it a sandworm, bloodworm, or tapeworm, that won't arouse the interest of a bottom feeder.

Among surf anglers you'll find two schools as to the most productive technique. Sides are equally divided between casters who prefer using lures and those who like to fish with natural bait. I doubt if there's really an answer. Over many years of walking the beaches from Maine to Florida, I've balanced my fishing between the two.

Squid

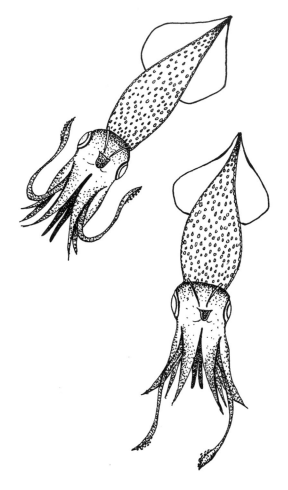

The squid family is composed of numerous 10-armed cephalopods, having a long, tapered body and a caudal fin on each side. Of the 10 arms, 2 are tentacles that are long and retractile, which enables them to seize food. They're white and firm, which makes them a fine hook bait. Along the surf they're used in a variety of ways, including as bait when cut into strips, chunks, or whole, or just the head section with its 10 trailing arms. The squid is much like the octopus, with the latter having eight arms and also being a fine bait.

The majority of squid used as bait are purchased frozen in packages, and range in length from 6 to 12 inches. I frequently purchase squid at a local fish market, where fresh squid are an Italian seafood delicacy.

Squid are a fine hook bait for many surf species. When the body is cut into 3- to 6-inch-long by 1/2-inch-wide strips, they're ideal for fluke and sea trout. Smaller strips may be used for kingfish, spot, and croaker.

The two-hook Sneaky Pete rig developed by Ernie Wuesthof is ideal when used with strips of squid. The favored technique is to place the lead hook near the head of a strip, with the rear hook in the strip's center. Cast out and slowly retrieve along the bottom; you'll receive strikes from summer flounder and southern flounder that work along the surf line as they feed on sand bugs, crabs, and sand eels exposed by wave action. Take care to lower your rod tip during the retrieve so the rig works properly until it reaches the sand; you'll often receive strikes just a few feet from where you're standing.

Whenever I cut strip baits from squid, I retain the heads for later use when I'm targeting stripers. When used on a one- or two-hook bottom rig with a float on the leader suspending the squid head off the bottom, it makes a very effective and enticing bait. Place the hook through the head so the arms and tentacles hang free. Suspended off the bottom, the wave action gives the squid head a life-like appearance. You'll find that stripers, bluefish, weaks, and redfish will readily respond to a whole squid head, as will sandbar sharks and spiny dogfish, plus skates and bullnose rays.

If the squid are small you can use a whole one, hooking it with a two-hook rig. Place one hook near the pointed end of the squid between the caudal fins, and the second hook in the body of the squid near the head. The head, arms, and tentacles trail freely.

Some anglers use a heavy brine solution of half water and half coarse salt to cure their squid. Soaking overnight in brine hardens the squid meat, which is then less apt to be ripped from the hook than softer, fresh squid.

Surf Clams

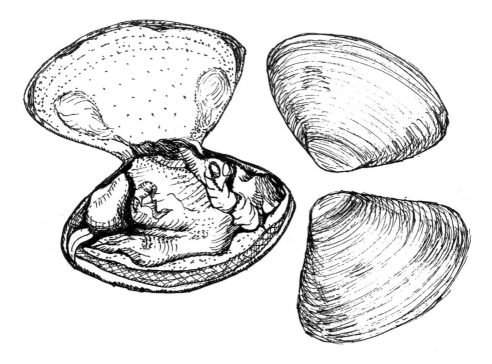

Surf clams might well be termed one of the best all-around baits that you can use to cast into the churning breakers. Having cleaned many species of fish caught from the beach, I've found clam meats in the stomachs of everything from striped bass to flounder, as well as bluefish and Spanish mackerel that are not normally thought to feed on the bottom.

The surf clam usually measures from 4 to 7 inches and is commercially harvested for canned chowder and clam strips. Commercial draggers supply bait shops along the coast as well.

You might wonder how a fish can eat a clam. Most often during a strong onshore wind and storm of several days' duration, the surf becomes extremely rough. Huge quantities of surf clams are exposed by the wave action, and literally carpet the ocean floor along the surf line. Many of the clamshells are broken open, and many species invade the surf to feast.

Other clams, some whole and others broken, are washed onto the beach. Exposed to the air, many of the whole live clams die, opening their shells as they expire. As the tide floods, the surf covers these clams, and stripers, weaks, spot, croaker, redfish, kingfish, and flounder all move in to feed.

Fresh surf clams can be easily shucked, and the clam meat and muscles along the edge of the shell removed for bait. The size of the bait should be tailored to the species being sought. The ribbonlike muscle is ideal when cut into 2- to 3-inch-long pieces and used for small fish such as spot, croaker, kingfish, and flounder. When larger species, such as stripers or redfish, are the target, cut the large piece of clam meat in half. Run the hook through a piece twice, adding several strips of muscle meat to hang freely.

Using surf clams as bait is usually most effective immediately after a storm, for that's when the surf species are feasting on the exposed and broken clams. Once the waters subside and all of the available clam meat has been consumed by both fish and crabs, the surf residents return to foraging on sand bugs, crabs, squid, spearing, sand eels, and other baitfish.

Immediately after a storm, I repair to the beach at low tide, where I walk along and collect a 5-gallon pail of clams for later use. I shuck the clams and place them in a heavy brine solution consisting of half coarse kosher salt and half fresh water. I store them in a 1-gallon plastic mayonnaise jar that I obtain from a local delicatessen. Once placed in the brine, the clam meat becomes very tough, and makes far more durable bait than fresh clams. I've regularly caught just as many fish on the salted clams as I do on fresh, and have kept them for months in my refrigerator with no loss of fish-catching quality.

Crabs and Sand Bugs

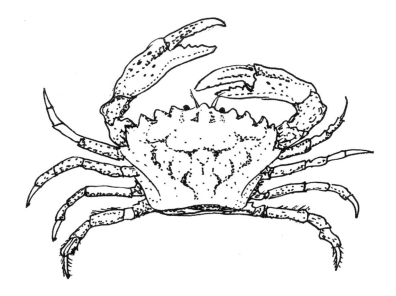

S everal species of crabs inhabit the surf or take up residence around rocky outcroppings and jetties. Joining them are sand bugs, called sand fleas along some sections of coast. At one time or another all become an easy meal for marauding bottom feeders and game fish.

The blue crab is perhaps the most popular crab along the coast and readily obtained in fish stalls or bait shops. Close behind is the calico crab, often called sand crab, which frequents the surf. Many surfcasters obtain their calico crabs using a crab rake fitted with a wire basket. At low tide the sand in the shallow surf is raked and the frisky crustaceans collected. Fiddler crabs and green crabs are also used while fishing from the surf and jetties, with both being very popular with anglers seeking tautog.

At one time or another I've found all of the above species of crabs and sand bugs in the stomachs of most of the fish I've caught from the surf and jetties. Summer flounder feed extensively on tiny crabs and sand bugs, some of which aren't much larger than your pinkie nail. I've counted more than two dozen of the tiny crustaceans in the stomach of a fluke, which was elongated to the size of a golf ball, so crammed with forage was it. I've found comparable quantities in striped bass and redfish. Even tiny spot, croaker, and kingfish feast on them.

Many of these crustaceans shed their shells more than 20 times before they reach maturity. Those having a hard shell can be used, but there's a consensus that a crab about to shed its shell is the best bait—it emits a scent that fish find attractive. Immediately after shedding its shell, and before it has a chance to harden, the crab is very soft, which makes a fine bait as well, although it's necessary to employ elastic thread to secure it to your hook.

Crabs may be used whole, or cut in small pieces, and fished on the bottom with a one- or two-hook bottom rig. I've often used the claws of soft crabs much as I would use a shrimp, worm, or piece of clam. You can secure the body of a large crab to your hook with elastic thread, letting the claws and swim fins hang freely.

Sand bugs seldom grow much longer than 2 inches, and impaling a whole bug on your hook works fine.

Anglers generally prefer shedder or soft crabs as bait, but I've found more hard crabs in fish than I have the soft or shedding kind, so don't hesitate to use them.

Crabs are very hardy and survive well even when out of the water. When you collect them, it's wise to break off the point of the claw, which will prevent them from nipping you. Keep them cool or covered with wet burlap and they'll stay alive for a day's fishing.

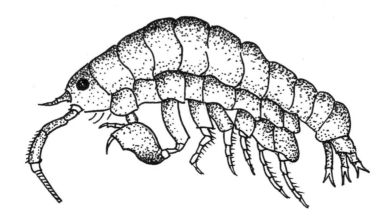

Shrimp

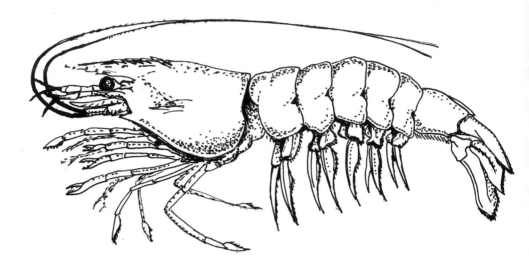

If you're a shrimp lover like me, it must hurt to think that you should use these tasty macrurous crustaceans as bait! Still, plentiful as they are along our shores, they have come to represent a sizable portion of the diet of many surf species.

I've encountered many anglers who fail to realize how plentiful shrimp are along the surf. Unlike baitfish, which can readily be observed as they swim about in schools, shrimp tend to hug the bottom or move through the mid-depths of the water column. My observation has been that from the Chesapeake Bay north to New England, the prevailing shrimp are the tiny grass shrimp, which measure but 2 inches at maturity and are thinner than a lead pencil. Many coastal bait shops primarily stock the tiny grass shrimp for use by boatmen, who use them as chum and hook bait while seeking weakfish and stripers. I've often used them as hook baits when spot, croaker, and kingfish are schooling in the surf and had fine results—enjoying a by-catch of fluke as well.

As you move from the Carolinas south to Florida you'll find large shrimp, any one of half a dozen species that measure from 3 to 6 inches in length, which are the same species used for shrimp cocktails and delicious scampi. Local bait shops carry the live shrimp, keeping them in aerated tanks. For a day's outing along the surf a couple of dozen of the lively shrimp are more than adequate, and may be kept alive in a 5-gallon pail. Make certain to change the water periodically so the shrimp don't die from lack of oxygen.

When hooked through the head, shrimp will stay alive and active, darting about enticingly. I've had especially good results while using a two-hook rig where each of the dropper loops holding the hooks has a small float on it, which suspends the shrimp off the bottom. Even when a shrimp expires on the hook, the fact that it's suspended by the float enables the current to move it about, within sight of any game fish or bottom feeder moving along the surf.

A trick I picked up while serving in the U.S. Marine Corps at Camp Lejeune, North Carolina, was to use pieces of shrimp as chum. We fished the broad expanse of New River inlet where it emptied into the Atlantic. On an ebbing tide we'd cut a shrimp into six or eight small pieces and toss them into a back eddy that formed where the river and ocean met. Spot, southern kingfish, croaker, spotted sea trout, and flounder would move in to feed on the shrimp chum, and we'd often wind up with a fine catch. Fortunately, the mess sergeant enjoyed fresh fish, and he'd often prepare our catch for a late-evening repast that was certainly superior to the daily fare!

Sea Worms

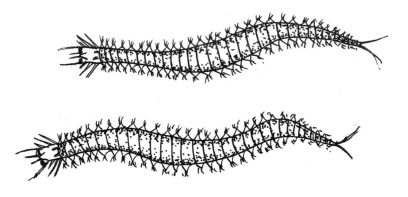

S ea worms can be found buried in the sand along the length of the Atlantic coast. Many are so small as to be impractical to use as bait, while others, such as the tapeworm, don't lend themselves to easily being harvested and shipped to bait purveyors. As such, other than the limited number of anglers who harvest their own, the majority of sea worms sold commercially are bloodworms and sandworms. Bloodworms are the smaller of the two, averaging 6 to 8 inches long, while sandworms often grow to a foot or more.

The greatest number of bloodworms and sandworms are harvested in Maine and airfreighted to coastal bait dealers. You can, however, dig your own by using a pitchfork at low tide to turn over the exposed mud and sand. I've even worked a pitchfork in shallow water with fine results, picking the wiggling worms from the sand and mud.

Not surprisingly, the first striped bass I ever caught, way back on May 16, 1946, inhaled a tapeworm bait fished on the bottom. I mention this because if you dig your own worms, you'll often encounter the tapeworm—a fine bait that has a pale sand color and is a foot or more in length.

Sea worms are usually shipped in cardboard boxes, packed with moist rockweed, and kept under refrigeration. I've kept them in the refrigerator at 40 degrees for up to a week, and suspect they'd last even longer. It's important, however, to turn the box daily, which keeps the worms active and prevents them from bunching up on the bottom and expiring. It seems that bloodworms survive longer than sandworms; the latter often tend to break apart after a couple of days. All sea worms tend to shrink in size over time. It's really best to purchase just what you feel you'll use for a day of surf fishing.

Bloodworms are the more durable hook bait. When using a whole worm for striped bass, weakfish, or redfish, insert a baitholder-style hook through the center of the worm, threading it onto the hook for an inch or so and permitting both ends to hang freely. When small surf species such as winter flounder, spot, kingfish, or croaker are your target, thread a 2- to 3-inch-long piece of worm onto the hook and let one end hang freely.

Sandworms are a very active hook bait. They're a favorite of surf anglers who target striped bass and weakfish. A favorite method of hooking them is to wait until one opens its mouth, then insert the hook in the mouth, threading the worm onto the hook's baitholder shank, which allows it to swim about enticingly. If the worms are small, you can add a second one in the same manner.

Mullet

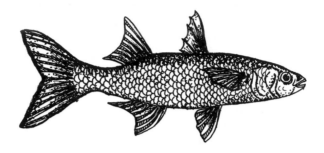

M ullet are found along the coast from Maine to Florida and are favored as a hook bait, either dead or alive. They spawn in coastal bays and rivers and usually spend most of the summer in warm, shallow waters. As autumn approaches, the mullet, which regularly congregate and swim together in huge schools often numbering 1,000 or more, begin a migration trek and then enter the ocean.

An ocean migration is something to behold. It's almost as though the mullet know that game fish and bottom feeders will be waiting for them. For as they leave coastal inlets, the tightly packed schools usually follow the contour of the jetty flanking the inlet, moving right around it, their huge mass clearly visible on the surface, and then moving in tight to the beach. There are times when they're immediately attacked, and thousands leap into the air simultaneously to avoid the marauders from below.

During this mass hysteria it's not unusual for mullet to swim so close to the beach that waves actually wash them high and dry onto the sand. With a receding wave they'll skitter back into the water, only to again be unmercifully attacked.

Along the northern coast it's striped bass, bluefish, weakfish, fluke, little tunny, and Spanish mackerel that feed ravenously on the helpless mullet, which range from 3 to 6 inches in length. Along the southern coast a whole new audience awaits their arrival as they vacate bay waters, including tarpon, snook, jacks, ladyfish, groupers, and snappers.

Within a day of the migration's start, coastal bait shops have fresh mullet available. Many surfing regulars carry a cast net during the fall, in anticipation of the mullet coming within range. One throw of the net, and you'll usually collect a 5-gallon pail of the silvery baitfish. You can place a nominal number of mullet in a bucket and they'll remain alive and well as hook baits. Package the remainder in ziplock bags or, better still, vacuum-pack them in Food Saver bags and they'll retain their freshness.

You can also use a snatch rig to obtain mullet. Simply cast just beyond the school and vigorously work your rod tip as you retrieve, which will quickly impale one. You can often score by simply permitting the mullet to settle to the bottom or swim about; a hungry game fish will quickly find it. You can also remove it from the snatch rig's treble hook and hook it through the lips or back as a live bait.

A favorite mullet rig consists of a red and white cork or Styrofoam float attached to a wire leader, which in turn is attached to a long-shank Carlisle-style hook. The hook is slipped into the mullet's mouth, out its gill, and then run through its back. The float suspends it enticingly.

Hickory Shad, Herring, and Mackerel

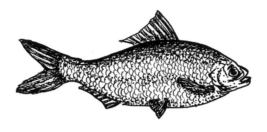

Hickory shad, herring, and mackerel are fine bait for a variety of surf species, but some are not normally available in coastal bait shops. You can catch your own, however, and you'll enjoy catching them as much as using them for bait. They move along the surf in sizable schools and respond readily to tiny shad darts or Sabiki rigs. I've hooked many that assaulted the 2/0 Clouser I often use as a teaser ahead of my primary lure. When hooked on a lightweight spinning outfit, they give a good account of themselves—the larger hickories and mackerel often weigh a couple of pounds. Hickory shad and blueback herring also jump repeatedly when hooked.

Each of these species can be fished as a live bait from the surf, especially when you're seeking heavyweights such as striped bass, tarpon, or bluefish. They may be hooked lightly through the back just forward of the dorsal fin, and cast from coastal jetties. From the surf you'll get best results by using a breeches buoy rig, which enables you to present the bait well off the beach without actually casting the live bait itself.

All of these species also make excellent hook baits when fished as chunks. I'm especially fond of the head section of the bait, which I cut off at a 45-degree angle, permitting the entrails to remain as part of the bait. I usually place the hook in the bait's lips and fish it from a bottom rig with a float on the leader, which suspends the bait off the bottom. I use the head because it's more difficult for crabs to rip this from the hook than is the case with softer body sections. However, the remaining body and tail section of a hickory, herring, or mullet can be cut into appropriate-sized chunks with equally good results. To help the bait stay on the hook, I'll often take several wraps of elastic thread after baiting up.

All of these baits can be filleted, and the fillets then cut into strip baits. They're especially effective when fished with a Sneaky Pete rig for fluke. I cut them anywhere from 3 to 5 inches long by 1/2 inch wide. Take care not to cut the bait too wide. Many anglers make this mistake, and the end result is a hook point resting against the wide strip. This often leads to missed strikes, because the point becomes embedded in the bait and slips out of the fish's mouth.

Spot, kingfish, croaker, and sea trout often respond to small pieces of these species fished on a two-hook bottom rig cast just beyond the breakers.

Should your targeted species fail to cooperate, don't fret: Hickory shad, herring, and mackerel all make fine table fare. Many anglers fillet and lightly sauté them. They're also great when filleted and pickled.

Mummichog (Killie)

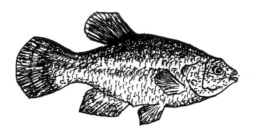

I 've never heard anyone call it that, but *mummichog* is the name of one of the most popular small live baitfish along the Atlantic coast. Most anglers throughout its range call this hardy baitfish the killie or minnow. The size favored by anglers ranges from 2 to 3 inches, although I've seen adult mummichog that measured a full 5 inches.

Of the various live baits used by surf anglers, killies are most readily obtained at coastal bait shops, where they're sold by the pint. Extremely hardy, they'll stay alive so long as you replace the water in your bait bucket regularly, thus maintaining a good level of oxygen.

Killies are found in most coastal bays and estuaries, and range into brackish and even fresh water. You can easily obtain your own by using a small seine and drawing it through shallow water along marsh grass and sod banks. Killies often linger in the shallows, where they can seek sanctuary among the marsh grass.

Another effective method of obtaining killies for a surf outing is to place a killie trap in waters they frequent. Use a piece of clam, mossbunker, or other fish, and after a couple of hours in the water you'll have all the killies you'll ever need for a day of surf fishing. I even have a few friends who keep a saltwater aquarium for their excess killies, and thus always have a supply available.

While transporting them to the fishing grounds, it's best to keep killies in a bucket of seawater. You can also transport them in a bed of rockweed that is kept wet.

Most often my target species when using killies from the surf is summer flounder. I use a basic bottom rig with a Claw- or Beak-style hook, and lightly hook the killie through the lips; it remains alive and frisky for a long while. A favorite technique is to cast just 100 feet or so and slowly retrieve the killie along the bottom. Flounder will often grasp the killie, and it's important when you feel the strike to refrain from the urge set the hook. Instead, just keep reeling; as the flounder feels the killie attempting to get away, it bites down all the harder and is hooked in the process.

Over the years I've caught practically all surf species on live killies. The majority—including such species as striped bass, weakfish, and bluefish—were caught while I was targeting summer flounder. They're extremely effective, so it may come as a surprise that not too many anglers employ them from the beach. I suspect it's because of the inconvenience of obtaining and transporting these energetic little fish.

Atlantic Silverside

The Atlantic silverside represents an important link in the food chain upon which species that frequent the Northeast surf thrive. It has a near-transparent green coloration along its back, blending into a silvery band along its sides, and a white belly. Silversides are found along the surf throughout the year, but they're especially prevalent during early fall and winter as they vacate the protected reaches of bays and rivers where the juveniles are hatched in early summer.

As the silversides move into the ocean they do so in large schools. Many seek sanctuary among the rocks of coastal jetties, especially at inlets. Others hug the shallow water along the sand, in the troughs inside the sandbars. I've been on the beach on a quiet November night with an offshore wind and dead-calm surf; I could hear thousands of frightened silversides fluttering on the surface as they attempted to avoid an onslaught from striped bass. I've observed the same while fishing from jetties, with many thousands of the 3- to 4-inch-long baitfish packed tightly against the rocks in the hope of avoiding the jaws of hungry stripers, blues, and weaks.

The Atlantic silverside is popularly called spearing throughout most of its range. Unfortunately, it's very difficult to net spearing and keep them alive. Most are commercially netted and then frozen. As such, anglers using them don't catch the very species that most often feed on silversides.

Spearing rank as one of the most popular baits used while fishing for summer flounder from the beach. They work best with a two-hook rig: Run the lead hook through the head or eyes of the spearing, and the trailing hook through the rear of the body. Hooked in this manner, the bait can be cast out and retrieved slowly yet erratically along the bottom. Fluke are often feeding within a couple of rod lengths from the sand, and it'll feel as though you've snagged bottom when they first mouth the bait. Avoid striking prematurely. I've found it best to just keep reeling, which results in the fluke biting down harder—and getting hooked in the bargain.

Spearing are also very effective when bluefish and weakfish are plentiful along the surf. The mullet float rig can be used with spearing, hooking one or two of them on the two-hook rig as described above for the bottom rig. The float on the rig will suspend the silverside off the bottom, where the wave action will tumble it about and make it enticing to any surf species.

While silversides are primarily a baitfish, if you obtain your own using a seine or cast net and have surplus at day's end, you'll find they're a gourmet treat when deep-fried whole.

Bay Anchovy

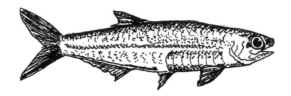

There are nine species of anchovies that populate the waters of the western Atlantic, many of which are so similar that it takes a trained scientist to distinguish among them. The bay anchovy is one of the most common, as it populates the waters of bays and rivers in its infancy, then moves into the open ocean and along the surf as it reaches maturity. A close cousin, the striped anchovy, has much the same habits, and often huge schools of the tiny forage are found in the same coastal range.

The bay anchovy is included here because it constitutes a major forage species found along the surf, although because of its tiny size it seldom becomes a hook bait.

The anchovy family features a wide, underslung mouth. Its single dorsal fin distinguishes it from the Atlantic silverside, which has two dorsal fins. Anchovies are tiny, usually from 1 to 3 inches in length, although some species do grow to 5 or 6 inches. Most have a brilliant silvery color, with a bright silver lateral line. They are nearly translucent, which has resulted in their being called glass minnows and rainfish throughout much of their Atlantic coast range. They are generally not available in bait shops but can be obtained with a cast net in the surf.

While they constitute a major forage species for the game fish and bottom feeders that frequent the surf line, their presence is enough to give surfcasters fits. Rainfish travel in huge schools, often numbering in the thousands. It's a sight that causes the heartbeat of casters to accelerate, especially when bluefish, striped bass, weakfish, little tunny, and other surf residents attack them from below. It is not at all uncommon to see literally thousands of bay anchovies leap into the air simultaneously to avoid the hungry predators. They're also attacked from above, as the sky is often darkened with gulls and terns beyond count, which congregate to enjoy an easy meal.

You might think this an opportune time to score, but because anchovies are so small—many just an inch or two long—the feeding game fish are often so intent on inhaling mouthfuls of anchovy that they ignore any large plugs, leadheads, and tin you cast their way.

When I encounter this situation I often score with teasers—as described elsewhere in this book—fished ahead of a primary lure. Use a teaser that's chartreuse and white, with several strands of silvery Mylar, and often you'll receive immediate strikes. I've also had fine results while fly casting a Clouser Minnow, a Deceiver, or especially a Bob Popovics Surf Candy.

American Sand Lance

A s with so many species of baitfish, the American sand lance has more than one name; it's known more commonly as a sand eel or sand launce. Whatever it's called, though, surf anglers are delighted when this long, thin baitfish invades the surf: There are certain to be many game fish and bottom feeders close at hand, for they know an easy meal is in the offing.

Superficially, the sand lance resembles an eel, but it can easily be distinguished by its separate instead of continuous dorsal, anal, and caudal fins. It has a brownish back and silvery white belly. The majority of sand eels encountered along the surf range from 3 to 6 inches in length, although 8-inchers are not uncommon.

Sand eels travel in dense schools, numbering in the thousands. I've often snagged them on the treble hooks of a plug as I cast along the beach, so densely were they packed.

I suspect the name *sand lance* is derived from their ability to burrow into the sand, often to a depth of 6 inches. As you walk along the surf, you can readily observe them beneath the sand. When a wave recedes, the sand eels squirm along beneath the surface of the sand, their profiles clearly slithering along. Often dozens of them can be observed, squirming parallel to each other as a wave recedes. It's their way of avoiding the variety of game fish and bottom feeders that are searching for an easy meal. While raking for calico crabs along the surf, I've often raked up handfuls of buried sand eels. I've also exposed them as I used a pitchfork to dig for clams.

Sand lance are easily obtained as bait by using a cast net from the beach; the big schools are often close to the sand, particularly at dusk and daybreak. They're also available frozen at most coastal tackle shops.

They're extremely effective bait for summer flounder when these flatfish exit bays and rivers in the fall. At that time the fluke move along the surf, feeding extensively on the sand eels. Fish them on a two-hook Sneaky Pete rig that you cast just beyond the breakers and retrieve slowly. The fluttering spinner blade of the rig acts as an attractor that readily brings strikes.

Sand lance also work very well when fished on a mullet float rig. The advantage of the float is that it suspends the bait off the bottom and away from crabs. It also gives the bait action as the surge of the surf swirls it about just off the bottom. Fished in this manner, a whole sand eel threaded on the rig will bring strikes from striped bass, weakfish, bluefish, and fluke.

Sand eels are also effective when cut into small pieces and fished on a two-hook bottom rig for croaker, kingfish, and spot.

American Eel

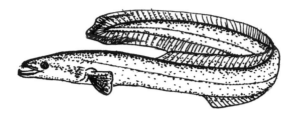

The American eel has an almost snakelike appearance as it slithers along the bottom of coastal creeks, bays, and estuaries. Having spawned in the Sargasso Sea in the western North Atlantic, the elvers—as the small eels are known—often travel 1,000 or more miles to reach brackish water. Predominantly an olive or dark brown to black color, they're plentiful in Atlantic coast waters year-round.

Eels in the 7- through 18-inch length are favored by anglers and can be purchased live at most coastal bait and tackle shops. I've often seined small eels along the marsh banks of coastal bays and rivers. Many anglers who favor them as bait set out eel traps; these permit the eel to slither into the trap, but prevent it from exiting. The traps, which I've used from my dock in Mantoloking, capture eels of all sizes. I keep the small ones as bait; the larger eels, some fully 3 feet long, are delicious, and can be pickled, smoked, or prepared using a variety of recipes.

Unlike many types of live bait, which expire quite easily, eels survive for a long while even when removed from the water. They may be kept in moist seaweed or rockweed at a cool temperature, and stay active for hours.

Live eels are a favorite bait of striped bass anglers who ply the surf. Surprisingly, while I've caught many stripers on both live and rigged eels over a span of many years, I don't recall ever having found an eel in the stomach of a striper. It might well be that stripers and other game fish will never pass up an eel—a delicate treat that they don't often encounter. I suspect the stripers that feed in brackish water are more apt to regularly encounter eels than those that ply the surf.

Fishing live eels from the beach is most often a cast-and-retrieve proposition. A 3-foot-long leader is used, with a single 6/0 or 7/0 O'Shaughnessy- or Live Bait–style hook. The hook is inserted in the lower jaw of the eel and out the upper jaw, or else run through the eye sockets. Hooked in this manner, the eel may be cast for hours on end and will stay alive remarkably well. The key in casting a live eel is to hesitate before beginning your retrieve, so that the eel settles down near the bottom, and then to retrieve slowly and irregularly, which keeps the eel moving along enticingly. Dead eels may be fished in much the same manner, or rigged on a block tin squid, which imparts a swimming action.

Bluefish attack eels with a vengeance, but frequently will chop an eel in half without getting hooked. I've seen anglers rig a stinger hook well back in an eel using a piece of stainless-steel cable or leader wire, which gets the short strikers. Weakfish, especially tiderunners, will readily strike eels, as will channel bass.

Menhaden (Bunker)

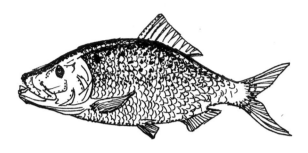

The menhaden, popularly called mossbunker or just plain bunker throughout its Atlantic coast range, is perhaps the single most important forage species for surf fishermen. The commercial fisheries harvest more than 2 billion pounds annually, which gives you some idea of how plentiful this species is. Primarily a plankton feeder, the menhaden spawns in coastal bays and rivers and is found from Nova Scotia to Florida.

Adult menhaden range from 1 to 2 pounds in weight and often migrate right along the surf in huge schools. They are easily snagged with a snatch rig and used live as bait for species such as striped bass, bluefish, channel bass, and tarpon.

During the early fall juvenile menhaden that were spawned in the spring begin to exit bays and rivers in huge schools. Popularly called peanut bunker, the schools travel south toward warmer climes. As they do so, the schools, often numbering thousands upon thousands of 4- to 5-inch-long fingerlings, are so close to the beach that waves will actually strand some of them on the sand.

This fall migration of peanut bunker is awaited by surf anglers all along the coast, for game fish such as striped bass, weakfish, bluefish, little tunny, tarpon, channel bass, and tarpon swarm into the surf to feed on the helpless fry.

For anglers who prefer to use lures, plugs such as the surface swimmer, popper, darter, Rat-L-Trap, and mirror plug all produce results. Casters often enjoy extraordinary results by using a snatch rig, which they cast beyond a school of surfacing menhaden and retrieve with a violent yanking of the rod tip, with the treble hook of the rig impaling the bait. The bait need not be retrieved, for you'll often receive a strike as the rig settles to the bottom: The menhaden emits distress signals as it struggles to free itself from the hook, which in turn attract game fish to the helpless fry.

Still another technique to try after you've used a snatch rig to obtain live bait is a breeches buoy rig. This enables you to present a large or small bunker several hundred feet from the beach.

Chunks of bunker are also very effective hook baits. I much prefer a chunk that includes the head; when fished on a bottom rig, this resists the onslaughts of pesky crabs, which have more difficulty removing it from your hook as it rests on the bottom. Chunks of the very oily bunker are especially effective because the pungent scent attracts a multitude of bottom feeders, from tiny spot to huge sandbar sharks, and almost anything in between.

CHAPTER 7

Bait Rigs

In this chapter you'll find a selection of rigs used by surf anglers to present different baits under a range of conditions. There are many variations of these rigs, with anglers in each area tweaking the rig to accommodate local baits for presentation to the species most often encountered along their particular stretch of surf.

The key to preparing all of these rigs is simplicity. Keep it simple, with a minimal amount of hardware associated with the rig, and you're apt to be more successful. Often these overbearing terminal rigs are made to look impressive, and as a result command a higher price. They're usually not as effective as a hand-tied rig, or one purchased at a local tackle shop.

I tie almost all of the rigs illustrated. Practice the knots illustrated herein, and you can tie up a batch of rigs in a couple of evenings that will last you all season long. I pack them individually in small ziplock bags or sandwich bags.

Don't hesitate to experiment with rigs. Just last season I made up a unique leader rig with a pair of teasers. It worked extremely well on small bluefish and weakfish. Likewise with the two-hook bottom rig; I made the loops longer so I could put a float on the loop, which resulted in both batis being suspended off the bottom.

Toward this end I've found the floats beneficial, in that they keep the baits away from crabs. More importantly, instead of a fish having to inhale the bait off the bottom, it can observe it floating enticingly in the current, then swim up and inhale it with ease. Next time out when there's a calm surf, place your bait rig in the water, and watch how it rests listlessly on the bottom. Then attach a small cork or Styrofoam float to the leader, and see how the bait suddenly comes to life as the current moves it about.

Breeches Buoy Rig

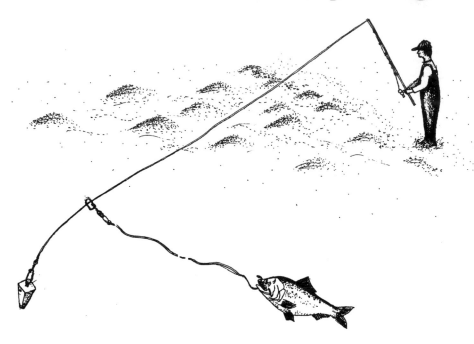

From Maine to Florida large game fish roam the surf, all of which will readily respond to a properly presented live bait. Among them are tarpon, striped bass, weakfish, channel bass, bluefish, and snook. The problem surf anglers encounter is casting a live baitfish that weighs a pound or more beyond the breakers, and then keeping it there.

Years ago I was introduced to the breeches buoy rig while fishing in Florida. Anglers fishing from both piers and the beach used it to present live mullet to big king mackerel. The rig employed the same breeches buoy principle once used to move shipwrecked people from their craft on an outer bar to shore. I also saw it used for transferring mail from destroyers to troopships.

TYING THE RIG

The first step in making up a breeches buoy rig is to prepare a leader, which should be geared to the size of bait you're using. For presenting an adult menhaden, horse mullet, or croaker, you'll need about 3 feet of 30- or 40-pound-test fluorocarbon leader material. Snell a Claw-, Beak-, or Live Bait–style hook in 6/0 or 7/0 size, or a 10/0 or 12/0 Circle hook, to the end of the leader. Then use a uniknot to tie a barrel swivel or ball-bearing swivel with a coastlock snap to the other end. Double several feet of the terminal end of your line using a surgeon's loop, and use a uniknot to tie a large duolock snap to the end of your line. Then snap a pyramid-style sinker to the end of your line.

FISHING THE RIG

Here's where we depart from the norm. Cast your sinker to the area where you want your live baitfish to be—in a break between the bars, in the trough inside the bar, or just in deep water well off the beach. Yes, cast without the leader attached.

Next take a live herring, mullet, menhaden, mackerel, hickory shad, croaker, or other live baitfish, and hook it through either the lips, the eye sockets, or the fleshy part just forward of the dorsal fin. Open the coastlock snap attached to the leader, slip it onto your line, and close the snap.

Lift your rod tip high in the air, and the coastlock snap, leader, and baitfish suspended from it will slide down the line and into the water, where the baitfish will most often begin to swim in the line of least resistance, which will be toward the sinker.

Then patiently sit back and wait for a strike. Sometimes you'll see the baitfish swim back toward you, perhaps fluttering about on the surface where the line enters the water. This is often a result of its being stalked by a big fish, which the little bait excitedly tries to avoid. When a fish finally does take the bait, the coastlock snap will come tight against the duolock snap and sinker—and by that time the hook has usually struck home.

Snap Float Live-Bait Rig

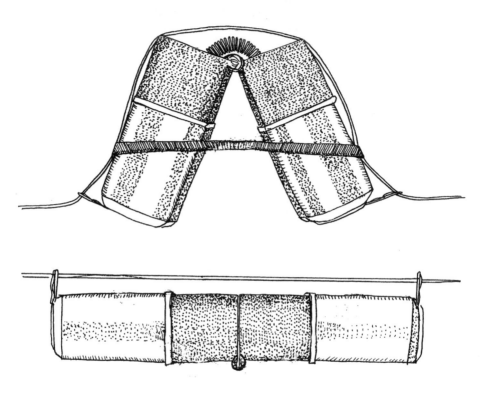

The Snap Float is a unique float developed by Jim Kaczynski and was initially designed for use on the offshore grounds while fishing with big baits for sharks and tuna. Its unique design enables you to slip it onto your line, then set it at the desired position by bending it open and attaching an elastic band. This holds the float in position until a strike is received. Upon receiving a strike, the float snaps shut and the elastic pops off, with the float sliding on the line as you fight your fish.

FISHING THE RIG

Anglers fishing the barrier islands of Virginia and along Carolina's Outer Banks often fish for sandbar sharks from the surf. They've found the Snap Float ideal for presenting their big live baits to cruising sharks.

The only catch is that you need an offshore wind—the wind at your back—to literally blow the Snap Float and bait suspended from it seaward, much as the wind would propel a piece of driftwood seaward.

If there's no wind but a moderate current is moving along the beach, the rig may also be used, providing there aren't too many anglers on the stretch of beach you plan to fish. In this situation the bait is suspended on a leader 4 or 5 feet beneath the float and cast a moderate distance. A long cast usually isn't possible due to the weight of the float and bait. You then move along the beach as the current carries the float and bait along.

If you're fishing where there are offshore bars, you'll note that when you come to a break in the bar, usually called a hole or cut, the current is usually exiting through the break. This is often called a rip tide, for the waves that crash across the bar then move parallel with the beach, forming the current, which then travels seaward as it reaches the break.

Often the Snap Float and bait will be carried seaward through the deep hole, which is where striped bass, channel bass, sharks, bluefish, and other surf species take up residence to feed.

The Snap Float rig also works extremely well when fished from coastal jetties. Along most stretches of surf there's a current running parallel. When this current reaches a rock jetty, groin, or breakwater that extends seaward, the current moves parallel with it, then around the front of it, and continues on down the beach.

You can easily experiment with a couple of casts until you determine the flow of the current, and then position yourself so that the current carries the Snap Float and its suspended bait. Often game fish, especially stripers, will take up station at the seaward end of the jetty, waiting for the current to carry a meal to them. Properly positioned, your Snap Float rig will do just that.

Mullet Float Rig

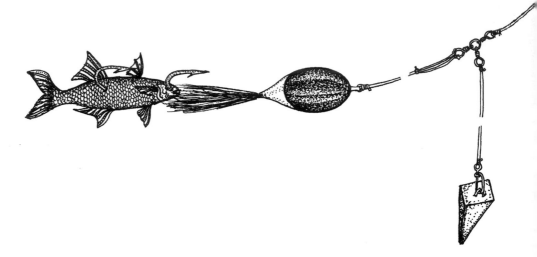

Mullet and bluefish go together like peanut butter and jelly. Few would question that the single most popular rig for presenting a mullet in the surf in the hope of catching a bluefish is the mullet float rig. While its name implies that it's a rig to be used with mullet, it can also be used with a variety of other baits. Although its popularity centers on bluefish, it's equally effective on many species. It's a versatile rig that has a wide range of applications.

RIG VARIATIONS

There are many variations on the mullet float rig available in coastal tackle shops, each with nuances felt by its designer to enhance its fish-catching ability. The basic rig consists of a very long-shank Carlisle- or O'Shaughnessy-style hook, with a small egg-shaped Styrofoam or cork float attached to its shank near the eye. The float is usually painted red and white, although other color combinations are available. A tuft of feathers or bucktail is tied to the shank of the hook. The eye of a smaller hook is opened and slipped around the shank of the primary hook, where it swings freely in the bend of the J-style hook. The rig is completed by tying it to a 30- to 36-inch-long piece of fluorocarbon leader material, with a small three-way swivel and a connecting link or a short piece of monofilament to accommodate the pyramid-style sinker.

A variation on the rig includes a removable hook that is attached to a short wire leader haywire-twisted to the float. This enables you to insert the wire through the bait, slip the double hook onto a loop in the wire, and pull the hook back into the bait. This positions the bait a couple of inches from the float. There are many other variations on the rig, with the primary emphasis on positioning the bait so a toothy bluefish can't bite through the short wire leader or the pair of hooks.

FISHING THE RIG

The most popular way of placing a mullet on the basic mullet float rig is to place the primary hook through the lips or eye sockets of the mullet, and then run the trailing hook through the back of the mullet near the tail. When a bluefish takes the bait, it usually attempts to bite it in half, as bluefish are prone to do. It then gets hooked on the trailing, or stinger, hook near the tail.

You can use a variety of baits with this rig, including peanut bunker, spearing, sand lance, or a strip of squid. Over time I've caught practically every fish imaginable on this rig, from heavyweight stripers to tiny spot.

The mullet float rig effectively presents the bait off the bottom, where the movement of the current and waves keeps moving it about a couple of feet off the bottom. The feather or bucktail skirt provides a tantalizing movement around the bait that any surf species searching for a meal finds irresistible.

Bait-Snagging Rig

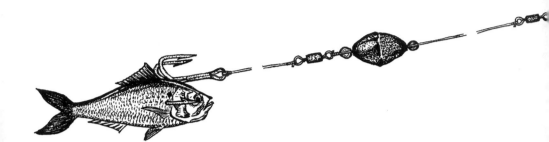

Nothing is more frustrating than repairing to your favorite stretch of surf and suddenly seeing a school of baitfish appear in front of you—but having no way to obtain one for use as a live bait.

Forage species such as hickory shad, herring, mackerel, mullet, menhaden, and others often move along the surf in huge schools. Quite frequently there are schools of stripers, blues, weakfish, little tunny, or other game fish close on their heels, for an easy meal is in the offing.

It's times like this when you wish you'd brought a bait-snagging rig along! It's an easy rig to tie. All you need are two 50-pound-test Spro power barrel swivels, a 1-ounce egg-shaped sinker, a sharp treble hook, and a couple of feet of 20-pound-test monofilament.

Cut a piece of the mono a foot in length. Tie a Spro swivel to the mono using a uniknot. Slip the egg-shaped sinker onto the mono and tie on the remaining Spro swivel. Tie another foot-long piece of mono to the Spro swivel. Complete the rig by tying the treble hook to the mono.

When you observe a school of baitfish in the surf, you can simply cast the snagging rig beyond the school and retrieve it with a vigorous sweeping motion of your rod tip. With luck the treble hook will impale a baitfish. Some anglers simply stop reeling once they feel they've impaled a baitfish, and permit the rig to settle to the bottom. The baitfish will emit distress signals, and a cruising game fish often quickly zeroes in on it.

Another approach is to reel in the snagged baitfish and present it via a liveline method or via a standard bottom rig, or permit it to swim about using a breeches buoy rig. In each instance, presenting a lively hook bait will often bring immediate action.

Another technique I use in tying a bait-snagging rig calls for a duolock snap, Spro swivel, three treble hooks, and 4 feet of 20-pound-test monofilament. Begin by tying on the duolock snap. Approximately 1 foot from the snap, slip one of the treble hooks onto the mono and tie it within a dropper loop, pulling the loop tight to the eye of the treble. Repeat, tying the second hook into a dropper loop a foot from the first, and then tie the third hook into a dropper loop a foot from the second. Complete the rig by tying a Spro swivel to the end of the monofilament.

This gives you three treble hooks tied tightly within the dropper loops, so they don't swing freely. I usually attach a Hopkins Shorty to the snap for casting weight. Cast the rig beyond a school of baitfish, permit the Hopkins to settle, and use long, sharp sweeps of the rod tip as you retrieve. This draws the three trebles across the backs of the baitfish, impaling them. Surplus bait can be kept alive in a 5-gallon pail of seawater.

Single-Hook Rig

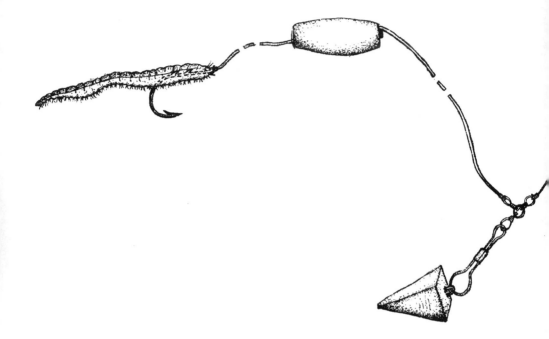

I can attribute many firsts of species caught from the surf to the single-hook rig. My first surf striper, fluke, weakfish, croaker, channel bass, and more all succumbed to a natural bait presented via a single-hook rig. Basically a very simple rig to tie and use, it does have several variations, each intended to present a natural bait as effectively as possible.

TYING THE RIG

The basic single-hook rig comprises a three-way swivel, connecting sinker snap, approximately 36 inches of fluorocarbon leader material of a test appropriate for the species being sought—15-pound test for weakfish, 30-pound test or heavier for stripers and redfish—and a hook of a size and style appropriate for the quarry.

A favorite hook style for bait fishing is the Claw or Beak style, with a barbed, baitholder shank that helps keep the bait from sliding down on the bend of the hook. Using this rig with small size 2 or 3 hooks works for spot, croaker, and kingfish, while 2/0 through 7/0 sizes are favored when using larger baits for species such as striped bass, redfish, or snook.

Size regulations are in effect for many surf species, and quite a few anglers along the beach have taken to using Circle-style hooks instead of the J-style hook. With the Circle hooks the fish are usually hooked in the corner of the jaw, which makes unhooking and releasing undersized fish less of a challenge. Keep in mind, however, that you have to move up to larger sizes—up to 10/0 or 12/0, for instance—where you'd be using a 7/0 J style.

To tie up a single-hook rig, tie the fluorocarbon leader material to the three-way swivel using a uniknot. The next step is to snell your hook to the terminal end of the leader. Place the connecting link sinker snap on the three-way swivel, attach a pyramid-style sinker of sufficient weight to hold bottom, and you're all set to bait up and cast out.

Some anglers prefer to minimize hardware, so instead of using a sinker snap they tie a short piece of monofilament to an eye of the three-way swivel and then tie a surgeon's loop, onto which they slip their sinker.

A good variation on this rig, and the one I frequently use, is to slip a 2-inch-long torpedo-shaped cork or Styrofoam float onto the leader, approximately 2 feet from the swivel. This suspends the bait 2 feet off the bottom, away from crabs but (importantly) still in view of any bottom feeder or game fish cruising along the surf.

FISHING THE RIG

When baiting up with whole sandworms, bloodworms, spearing, sand eels, or squid, you can simply slip the bait onto the hook. With clams or crabs, it often helps to use several turns of elastic string around the bait and tie it off. This helps secure the bait to the hook, and prevents it from pulling off as you execute a cast.

Multihook Rig

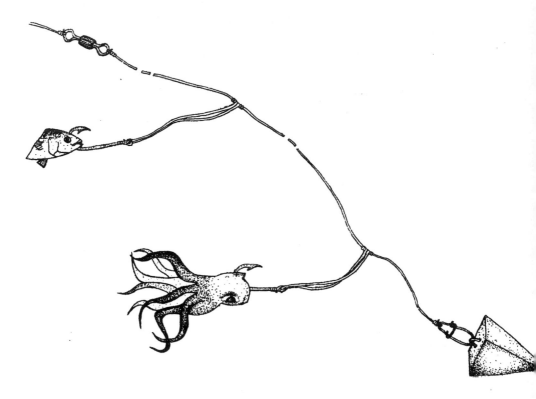

The multihook rig is designed primarily for the many small species that frequent the surf. It consists of a pair of Claw- or Beak-style hooks with barbed baitholder shanks, usually ranging from size 3 through size 8.

The hooks are snelled to approximately 12 inches of fluorocarbon leader material, and then one of the hook's leader is attached to the leader of the other. You can use a uniknot, blood knot, or dropper loop. Complete this by attaching a small three-way swivel, with the pyramid sinker attached via a connecting link sinker snap.

This rig may be used with 2- to 3-inch-long pieces of sandworm or bloodworm when winter flounder are entering or exiting river systems as they migrate. Often they linger in the inlets or along the surf to feed.

A variation is to begin with a 6-foot-long piece of 30-pound-test fluorocarbon leader material. Tie a small Spro barrel swivel to one end of the leader and a duolock snap to the other. Next, tie a dropper loop into the leader approximately 6 inches from the swivel; when closed, the loop should extend out about 8 inches. Repeat the procedure with a second dropper loop, this one tied 6 inches from the duolock snap.

I make up this rig in two different models, one to permit the baits to rest on the bottom, and the other suspending them. For the float rig, just slip cork or Styrofoam floats onto the dropper loop. This will cause the baits to float just off the bottom, which enables fish to inhale them with ease rather than having to root them off the bottom.

The final step in preparing the rig is to use a Claw- or Beak-style hook with a baitholder shank and turned-down eye. The hook size should take into account the species being sought and the bait being used. If you're using half a surf clam, a 6/0 or 7/0 Claw hook, or a larger Circle hook, is appropriate. If you're targeting croaker, kingfish, spot, and winter flounder, hooks ranging from 3 to 8 are fine.

To place the hooks on the dropper loop, slip one onto each loop. Do not pull them up tight. Instead, pass the hooks through a second time, which results in more bulkiness of the leader material. When pulled up tight, it holds the hooks tightly in place and prevents them from slipping down. I usually employ a pyramid-style sinker sufficiently heavy to hold in a heavy surf, but a dipsey or bank style can be used in a calm surf.

The advantage here rests with the sinker positioned at the terminal end of the rig. As you execute a cast, the sinker carries the leader, with dropper loops and baits trailing; this results in fewer tangles and longer casts. Tied properly, the hooks on both dropper loops are separated, so they can't tangle with each other.

Live-Bait Rig

The live-bait rig has brought me many memorable moments while casting with a variety of live baits, including the American eel, Atlantic herring, blueback herring, hickory shad, mullet, and menhaden. The catches range from huge tarpon and snook in Florida, to redfish along the barrier islands from Georgia to Virginia, to stripers, blues, and weaks on north to New England.

When I first began using it years ago, I tied a barrel swivel to the braided nylon line, followed by a leader and hook. Now if I'm casting with 15- to 20-pound-test line, I tie a surgeon's loop about 2 feet in length at the terminal end of my line. I next use a surgeon's knot to tie a 3-foot piece of 30- or 40-pound-test fluorocarbon leader material.

As an aside, while the surgeon's knot and loop are normally tied by looping the line twice, of late I've tried what is called a Venezuelan knot, which passes the looped end of the leader through the loop five times. It's important to wet the loop before pulling it tight, which results in a very neat, tight, strong knot that passes through the rod's guides with ease. The final step is to tie your hook to the end of the leader using a uniknot.

When targeting most of the aforementioned species and using baits that often weigh upward of a pound, large hooks are the order of the day . . . or night. Claw-, Beak-, or Live Bait–style hooks in sizes 5/0 through 7/0 are favored, although Circle hook fans often use 10/0 or 12/0 models.

Because I'm usually targeting striped bass, my favorite surf bait is a live American eel. Eels ranging from 6 to 18 inches may be used. I'll usually carry three or four secured in a plastic pouch with some wet rockweed.

The eel may be hooked through the lower jaw and out the upper, or through the eye sockets. To prevent the bait from slipping off the hook after repeated casting—when the hook hole is apt to expand—many anglers take a 1/4-inch-wide elastic band and cut it into 1/2-inch strips, with one slipped over the point of the hook. Cast out, permit the eel to swim toward the bottom, and then begin a slow, irregular retrieve.

With herring, menhaden, hickory shad, snapper bluefish, and other species, it's best to hook the bait through the fleshy part of the back just forward of the dorsal fin.

Using live baits requires patience, as well as room on the beach. Carefully, softly cast your bait—if you use the customary snap cast, you'll rip the bait from the hook. Once the bait is swimming on its own, permit the current to carry it along the beach, walking alongside with your reel in free spool or in the liveliner position. Often the bait will swim freely and even move a long distance from the beach. Keep minimal pressure on the line, so the bait has its freedom to move about.

Sneaky Pete Fluke Rig

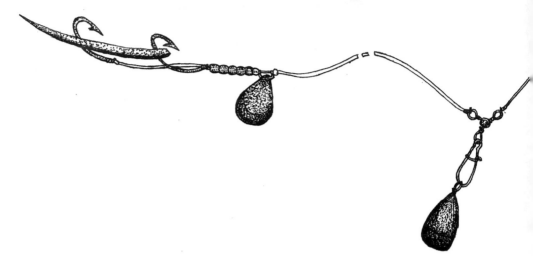

S ummer flounder, popularly called fluke in many areas, are noted for their habit of seizing a baitfish in their jaw. They'll often grasp it in their tooth-filled mouth just behind the hook, sometimes biting the bait in half.

When you're using a single hook, as many fluke anglers do, it has to be positioned at the head of the bait, so the bait doesn't spin. An alternative to hooking those short-striking fluke was to design a rig that presented a second, or trailing, hook positioned in the center of the bait, where the fluke is most likely down to bite down on it. Thus was the Sneaky Pete rig born.

There are many variations on the rig, with each tackle shop along the coast tying its favorite. From my observation Ernie Wuesthof of Normandy Beach, New Jersey, has done more to popularize this rig than anyone.

TYING THE RIG

The rig is easy to tie. Begin with a 3-foot-long piece of fluorocarbon leader material. Snell one Claw- or Beak-style hook in sizes 1 through 2/0 to the end of the leader. Then snell another hook to the leader, separated from the first hook by about 2 to 3 inches.

Next, slip four small red beads onto the leader, followed by a small Colorado-style spinner, followed by another bead. You can even use a small June Bug spinner if you wish. Tie the leader to a small three-way swivel. Add a small connecting link or duolock snap to one of the remaining eyes of the swivel—or you can use a small looped piece of monofilament, onto which you attach a 1- or 2-ounce dipsey-style sinker.

Tie the terminal end of your line to the remaining eye of the swivel, and you're set to bait up. I much prefer to use a strip bait with this rig, because a strip cut from a sea robin, dogfish, or sand dab is very tough and withstands repeated casting. Still, you can use spearing, sand eels, or squid as well.

FISHING THE RIG

Place the lead hook through the head section of the bait, and insert the trailing hook through the strip so that the strip lies flat and does not curl up on the hook. Cut each strip sufficiently narrow so that when the hook is placed in it and lies flat against it, the point extends 1/8 inch beyond the side of the strip. That way it isn't buried and is always in position to penetrate.

Fishing the rig is just a matter of casting out and slowly retrieving along the bottom. Vary the retrieve on alternating casts, sweeping the rig forward with your rod tip, reeling up the slack, and repeating until you find the combination that produces. Often a strike will feel as though you've snagged bottom, and it's important that you resist the temptation to strike. Just keep reeling, and momentarily the fluke will turn with the bait in its mouth. Invariably that second hook will be embedded securely in its jaw.

Fishfinder Rig

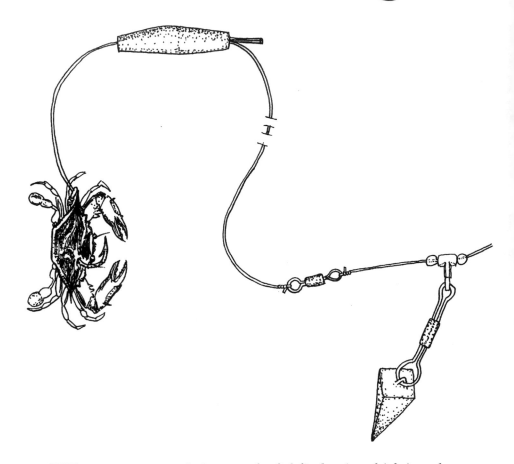

There are many variations on the fishfinder rig, which is perhaps the most basic rig of those used by surfcasters. It's a molded T-shaped piece of plastic, with a smooth hole through the top of the T, and a another hole at the bottom of the T onto which a duolock snap or connecting link is attached, to which in turn a pyramid sinker is attached. Your line is then slipped through the smooth hole at the top of the T.

Next, tie on a Spro power swivel or barrel swivel with an eye large enough that it cannot exit back through the hole, thus permitting the fishfinder rig to slide on the line.

To complete the rig, tie a 3-foot-long piece of fluorocarbon leader material to the Spro swivel. Slip a small Styrofoam or cork float on the rig approximately 24 inches from the swivel. Then snell a hook of your choice to the terminal end of the leader.

When seeking stripers, weakfish, channel bass, bluefish, and other larger surf species—including sharks, if you use a fine-wire leader instead of fluorocarbon—you can use a hook in sizes from 5/0 through 8/0, with a Beak or Claw style ideal.

This rig is especially effective with big baits. Often I'll use the head of an adult mossbunker or mackerel, a whole calico or blue crab, the meat of a whole surf clam, or the head of a squid with its tentacles hanging freely. When the rig is cast into the surf, the sinker holds the rig in place with the line taut, holding the swivel against the fishfinder rig.

The float on the leader suspends the bait, which is actually about a foot off the bottom. The current along the surf gives constant movement to the bait, enabling a hungry game fish to swim up to it and inhale it with ease.

The fishfinder enables the fish to turn after inhaling the bait and move off with it before swallowing. It works extremely well with the Penn Live Liner reel that I use while bait fishing. I have the liveliner lever activated, and as a big fish inhales the bait and moves off with it, the reel relinquishes line with minute drag pressure, enabling the line to slide through the fishfinder without ever feeling the weight of the sinker. When I feel that the fish has had sufficient time to ingest the bait, I lower the rod tip, flip the lever that activates the full drag, and lift back smartly to set the hook.

When targeting species covered by regulations, many anglers have begun using large Circle hooks. These usually grab in the corner of a fish's mouth, allowing an easy release. It's important to remember that with Circle hooks, you should employ a larger size than with J-style hooks. Where I would normally use a 7/0 J style, I'll move up to a 9/0 or 10/0 Circle hook.

CONCLUSION

You could say that this is the end. Hopefully, having read this far, you'll have a new comfort level in distinguishing between a sand lance and a spearing, or a darter plug and a popping plug. I would, however, say that whether you're a newcomer or veteran, this could be a beginning. For included within these pages is a wealth of information that I've gathered over many years of fishing not only the beaches of the Atlantic, but the Gulf and Pacific as well.

I say *a beginning* because to this day I continue to expand my knowledge. I'm often gathering a tip from another surf angler as to how he fishes a particular lure, or how she regularly scores with a home-tied bait rig.

The tackle, equipment, and techniques used while casting lures and baits are important. There's no question that the right outfit helps maximize your enjoyment of catching surf species. To me, however, surf fishing is more than just catching.

I still get goose bumps when I think of the day I cast into the rolling breakers, only to observe a seal raise its head from the water, almost questioning why I was there! It wasn't about to leave—I suspect it felt there was a meal in the offing—and its whiskered face popped up often.

Another time, in the half-light before dawn on a desolate beach, I vividly recall a fox sitting on the sand behind me, watching my every move. As I walked, he would walk, then sit with his ears erect as he observed me. He, too, was no doubt wondering what I was doing in his domain.

Then there were the countless sunrises. Did you ever stop to realize how few people have seen the sun rise on the ocean? No two sunrises are ever the same. They're gorgeous, and I enjoy every one of them.

As a full moon rises above the horizon, it brings light to the night like the sun brings light to the day. Few realize you can literally read a newspaper on those full-moon nights when there's not a cloud in the sky.

The real show often comes on the dark side of the moon. For in the pitch blackness the heavens come alive. There are stars beyond count, shooting stars, comets, and even satellites moving through the heavens.

You're exposed to nature's finest hour as you plod along, casting into the crashing surf, often showered with spray from an onshore wind. Suddenly you're brought back to reality with a heavy strike that practically rips the rod and reel from your grasp. With line screaming from your reel and a firm drag testing your mettle, you come to realize that surf fishing is really one of the most enjoyable, challenging, and contemplative pastimes you can participate in.

Join me out on the beach, and I guarantee you'll find it an experience that will bring you many rewarding memories that will last a lifetime.

INDEX